ABCs that make cent$

Tools needed to successfully climb your financial ladder to wealth

From

Cynthia Elliott, CPA

Cynthia E.

Keep climbing-
never stop; continue
to look up

authorHOUSE®

AuthorHouse™
1663 Liberty Drive
Bloomington, IN 47403
www.authorhouse.com
Phone: 1-800-839-8640

First published by AuthorHouse 10/26/2011

ISBN: 978-1-4634-4178-4 (e)
ISBN: 978-1-4634-3810-4 (hc)
ISBN: 978-1-4634-3811-1 (sc)

Library of Congress Control Number: 2011912759

Printed in the United States of America

This book is printed on acid-free paper.

Acknowledgements

Special Thanks To

This book would not have been published if it were not for the loving nudges from my mentor, Rutha Pegues, as I worked through the research and writing process. Her gentle but firm encouragement, guidance and support from the initial to the final product enabled me to push forward and complete what I set out to do: write this book.

If it were not for my next door neighbor, a true neighbor, Carolyn Michael-Banks, this book would have been held up by production costs. Her routine confirmations of calling me an author gave me hope as I would have placed a halt on publishing this book until my personal finances improved. I just forgot to include the cost in my budget.

Other Acknowledgements To

I offer my regards and blessings to others who supported me in any respect during the completion of this great and telling book: Gwendolyn Moorer-Garnett, Santhalyn Davis, Annie Chism-Conway, Anansa Bailey, Karen Madlock, Dee Dee Wike, Marie Horn, Eddie Jones, Russell Christy and Samuel Russell.

Pictures Taken By

I appreciate all of you for climbing the ladder (steps) in the 99 degree weather with full belief in the success of my book: Christina Elliott, Bob Willis, Janet Colbert, Elissa Pizza, Soinya Chaffen, Michael Stratton and especially Gerard Harts, the photographer.

In Loving Memory of my Mother
Evelyn M. Elliott (also known as 'Candy')
Who lived to be 88 years young

In loving memory of my mother, I honor all who suffer from the Alzheimer's disease also known as Dementia. Furthermore, I have the upmost respect for all of the personal conductors that soothe the Alzheimer's patients by saying, "Relax, I know who you are – it's okay if you don't." These words are to comfort the caregivers for their support, kindness and patience in providing for those who do not even know their next stop in life, not to mention their past journeys. Nevertheless, my mother who had Alzheimer's disease touched me by her gift of love and she touched others by offering her heart. I am able to love so deeply because of the huge sacrifices she gave up to provide for me and my siblings.

Thank you Butch for stepping up to the plate and taking charge;
You were such a wonderful care giver for our MOM.

In loving memory of my friends, Jeanette Blakeley and Janet Olsen, who inspired me to complete this finance book with a twist of a testament.

Foreword

"When are you going to write that book?" This was my frequent, nagging question each time I saw Cynthia Elliott for longer than I care to recall. "Soon," was the best response I could get, until now. "It's finished!" was the recent, welcomed response. The book I had been encouraging is the one we had discussed on many occasions: the down–to-earth, everyday guide to financial peace of mind. Finally! And yet, I must admit, there's never been a more opportune time for this indispensible guide through unfamiliar financial situations.

Through the many years I've known Cynthia, first as a student, then as a fellow CPA and friend, her talents and financial insights were readily apparent. I knew she had much to share if only she would commit her knowledge and experience to paper. That she would do so in the compelling and compassionate manner we see in this book is a Godsend.

> Trust in the Lord with all your heart, and lean not on your own understanding.
> Proverbs 3:5-6.

I write books myself. My Financial Accounting textbook is in its second edition. Its older sister, Intermediate Accounting is in its sixth edition. Both are published by McGraw-Hill/Irwin and are studied by university business and accounting students worldwide. Do these books show their readers how to manage their personal finances? No. Do they offer practical advice on spending, saving, budgeting, or managing credit. No. And neither do any of the many other accounting and finance textbooks. Cynthia's book, on the other hand, does all of these. But even more importantly, she guides us gently through these daunting areas of our lives in a comforting and reassuring manner with spiritual overtones. She is not preaching unpracticed techniques. She's been there, done that – and we feel that empathy throughout. We don't hope these suggestions work; we know they do.

This book is not a get rich quick guide. Instead, it's a practical plan to be rich with what we have, whatever that is. Life's journey is not about money. And yet, virtually all aspects of our lives have monetary implications. The fact that you are reading this book is a testament to your desire to better your financial understanding. You are about to embark on a voyage into monetary enlightenment. Enjoy your journey. You will be rewarded.

Prepared by J. David Spiceland, PhD, CPA
Professor of Accountancy

We can pat ourselves on the back for the increased lifespan of individuals living longer and sometimes even healthier. Now that we are living longer, we need to save more in order to have enough income during retirement. Therefore, we need to consider saving as early as childhood in order to be self-sufficient during our retirement years. If we are fortunate enough to obtain a job after schooling, we need to invest in ourselves and our future right away by setting money aside in the company's 401K plan and opening an account with an investment firm to make some profit and to accumulate wealth. Maintaining a retirement savings account is essential as well as saving for a 'rainy day' or unexpected financial challenges. Hardships are unforeseen and they tend to happen without any notice.

So what if you pay taxes on the profit you make from investments! Don't you think it is better to pay some taxes on your profit than to not make a profit at all? Let's live with the fact that you will pay some taxes. The focus should be on how to obtain extra funds for the special things in life, how to be financially ready for those rainy days and how to have adequate retirement money for just living in leisure. You know that your funds can accumulate over time. Your base investment is compounding daily from dividends and/or interests. It is the law of the 72-rule, which is a mathematical calculation. The general rule is that your funds will double around 7 years with the assumption that the interest rate is approximately 10%. You probably do not want another day to go by without saving a small percentage of your income. Don't wait until you are seven to the square root (49 years) before you understand and realize the importance of saving, time and the 'compound' effect on your money. Even if you are 50 years plus, it is better to save some late in life than to never save at all. You just need some time to see the effect of your dollars doubling and exploding. The key point to remember is before you are able to do anything significant and before you are able to do anything with pride, you will need to have money and to obtain money you need to save. So, let's start saving by setting aside a small percentage of your income TODAY; a good start will be 10% of your gross income.

Do you still need to be convinced? Do you think that you do not have enough money to save or to invest? What if I were to tell you that you do not need much in order to start saving. To open a savings account you may only need five dollars. Also, you need to regularly and consistently set money aside in an interest building account so that you can accumulate enough to work towards accomplishing your dreams. Do you have dreams?

Definitely, you will need to take some time out of your busy schedule to just DREAM. And, it's very important to write them down and work through them to fruition. Come on, you can do it! You are worth it! So what is your excuse now! For the sake of growing financially and personally, I would strongly recommend that you visit your favorite bank or investment firm and open up an account with a deposit that you feel comfortable with. Do not let another day pass by without investing in your future. In moving forward, make this book available for the whole family and allow it to assist you.

Prepared by the Author, Cynthia 'CENT' Elliott
www.ABCsthatmakecents.com

Over the past decade, America has been experiencing an economic crisis, the worst since the great depression in 1929. Most economists will agree that since the unfortunate events of 9/11, the American economy has been crippled. Even though it is unknown how long Americans will suffer, the financial experts agree that there are changes that must be implemented in order for America to rebound from this economic nightmare. My professional view is that we need to teach our children the benefits of implementing strong economic and financial values. I am confident that this book will provide just that opportunity to mold our children's financial direction with the assistance of their parents.

In order for America to avoid being exposed to such an economic crisis going forward, new methods and solutions must be imposed so that our country can sustain its historical front-running position, as it has possessed since its inception. There was a day when America was the model country when it came to economics, financial stability, low unemployment and a strong government. Now, America is almost at a stand-still; the experts cannot even predict the direction of our financial market. Is the economy going up or down?

Well, this book stimulated my interest because the author emphasized the importance of teaching our children the benefits of strong financial values. I concur it is crucial that we teach our children how to avoid the pitfalls we have encountered in the past, especially when it comes to economics and personal finances. Many of us as parents do a fine job in disciplining our children in reference to bad behavior but we have fallen short when it comes to financial discipline. If we are able to teach our children at a young age about the importance of good stewardship, then the future for Americans will be much brighter. I sincerely believe this because with proper guidance our children will make our country a better place. The children will not feel they need to keep up with the Joneses and try to live above their means. Our nation has been challenged because of the lack of discipline that we as consumers have demonstrated. Following the teachings of this book will help mold our children in the right direction. If this opportunity is missed while they are young, it will take much effort to make the change needed as an adult. It may be difficult but worth the effort. We must remember - we are our children's future. They are totally depending on us for direction and guidance. What we teach them today, will ultimately be what they will become tomorrow.

Now that we are rebounding from the 9/11 era and the aftermath that has been dumped on our door steps, let's begin to make wiser decisions as to the things that affect our economy. Not only is it important to make wiser decisions from our nation's capital standpoint, but we must make wiser decisions within our homes, schools and businesses. Just as Hillary Clinton has stated that, "it takes a village to raise our children," it also takes this country collectively to heal our nation financially and economically. So let's get started by challenging our families to make the changes noted in this book.

Now, I have had the pleasure of knowing Cynthia Elliott for over 15 years. Our business relationship began when she sought financial services and advice from me, as I am a financial services representative. Cynthia felt it was important to plan for her financial future and needed assistance with developing a plan to reach her short and long term financial goals.

Throughout the years, Cynthia and I have had many discussions concerning finances, the economy, politics and other important subjects that affect people's everyday way of life. I have found that Cynthia is a much focused, career-oriented individual. She is most certainly passionate about her work and a trailblazer in her industry.

From my dealings with Cynthia, I know her to be a very intelligent business woman with a professional attitude and presence. She has an impeccable background in accounting, and a knack for numbers. Cynthia utilizes the latest financial accounting programs and software and is proficient in many programs such as Quicken books and Microsoft Office among other leading computer software.

Being that America has experienced perhaps, the worst financial crisis in history, Cynthia's publication comes at a great time when people are in need of professional advice concerning their finances.

The information published in Cynthia's book is vital to anyone seeking knowledge in the finance field. Cynthia has hit a home-run with this publication. Cynthia is a visionary and when you combine Cynthia's financial accounting expertise and knowledge along with her tenacious personality, this is a recipe for a best-seller. I definitely recommend this book to people across America and around the world, as I am confident that this information will surely impact readers in a powerful way.

Prepared by Laurence V. Plummer, Sr.
President, Plummer Financial Services, LLC

Table of Contents

The Author's Personal Corner

I have always been amazed with folks attempting to teach others how to do something better or to teach others how to eliminate something completely, yet they have not experienced going through the tasks that they are teaching. Well, I am here to say that I have now gone through the challenges that I am currently writing about. Read below and learn of my personal journey regarding my limited finances during a difficult time in my life.

My first lesson:

Thou shall not write checks when you have no money in the bank.

While I was unemployed, I wanted so bad to continue to pay my mortgage. But, I had no money. When I first lost my job, I was not expecting any incoming funds right away since the unemployment process was slow getting started. Due to the economy, there were so many people experiencing the harsh reality of being unemployed. As a result, a great number of bills quickly began stacking up, in particular my mortgage. Let me tell you, before unemployment I was proud to say that I had excellent credit! I was known for paying my bills on time and for the full amount. When I became unemployed, I wanted to continue to uphold my good name. So, I would write checks, knowing that I did not have the money to cover even my routine expenses. The ironic part of it all was that I never got caught. Okay! Now the world knows, but somehow funds would come in just in time to cover those checks. The interesting part is that I was not expecting any incoming funds to hit my account. Would you call it luck? I called it a blessing! I remember doing a finance session on balancing the checkbook and how important it was to do so. Yet, I had not balanced my checkbook in months. Balancing my checkbook would have made it obvious that I had no money. I recognized that I was without a job, but I was not ready to accept that I was no longer receiving those twice a month direct deposits into my account to cover my expenses. Now, I understand why some individuals do not reconcile their bank accounts.

It can be depressing when all you see are negatives and you yearn, for example, to buy your daughter that $75.00 special white dress that is required for her group initiation ceremony. Sometimes I would write a check and hold it until one day before it was due and called the creditor to ask if they had received it. I definitely knew that they had not received the check because I had it in my hands. Because they had record of my credit history, that I paid my bills on time, the creditors would give me 'grace', allowing me that extra time needed to get my payments in to them. The question I had to ask myself was how long would I be able to continue doing this? Despite the way I was conducting my financial matters at the time, I do however teach how to manage during the difficult times using the appropriate tools accurately. My teachings have not changed; now I have a better understanding why folks without the funds do what they do. I am aware that folks do not purposefully write bad checks so that they can get charged by the banks a fee sometimes greater than the check amount and also get charged again by the creditors. This I do know, because I have been there and I have done that. But, please note that after the check bounces back into your hands, the creditors now do not trust you. You have lost that integrity for a long time to come and your credit rating may take a nose dive. Well, I had to finally accept that I did not have sufficient funds to pay all of my bills and I had to figure out other ways to manage through my current difficult state of unemployment. Blank checks, no money, and unemployment for over two years – this was my story.

Now, I want you to think about the times when you have gone out in the rain with a tiny umbrella or a broken umbrella. How do you cover up? Do you run and take cover or do you wait until the rain stops? I will discuss the many ways to not get drenched during the storm; you may get a little wet, but not soaked. In this book, I will mention various (appropriate and ethical) ways to 'cover' when a flood has saturated your finances.

My second lesson:

Thou shall not continue to live the life-style of the
rich and famous when you have no money.

Now, I understand when a couple gets a divorce, one may need to provide alimony to the other spouse due to a sudden change in life-style. Here I am unemployed, with a prior grand life-style of paying my essentials and eating out at least twice a week. This was my life-style. I was rich from the 'chocolate' and 'cheesecake' desserts. I was famous for eating at a fast-food restaurant on Fridays (for my daughter's sake) and some buffet style restaurant on Sundays after Church (for my benefit). Also, I kept up with the Joneses by keeping my yard cut weekly and getting my hair colored every other week. I was living it up…what a life I had. I had been working so many years, but in 2009 the company downsized, I was left without a job and those unemployment checks were not meeting my budget. I needed some extra funds so that I could maintain my life-style. I was suffering; I could no longer eat out. I ate salads without meat, not to mention not having my desserts and other special treats. I dare not mention maintaining my hair with the special treatment from a hair-stylist. I did not think about doing my hair myself. Remember I was used to going to a professional. I had no concerns for my yard; it looked okay to me. However, my neighbors disagreed. My grass got so high that one of my neighbors decided to cut it himself. I did not fret about my yard, but the decrease in funds was a big adjustment. I became depressed…I was hooked on my past life-style. Did I share with you that normally, I would purchase a new car, at least every 3-4 years? At the time, my car was 4 years old, operating well, but I felt like I needed a new car. I must tell you that my neighbor across the street just purchased a luxury car; I questioned God, why I had to continue driving my <u>used</u> car. How could I pull out the driveway daily and face my neighbor? I was extremely depressed. Now, I understood...things change, but people are slow to adjust to the change. Remember the phrase, "sacrifice now or sacrifice later." For the folks who have jobs, I teach how to sacrifice now and save for a rainy day. So when it comes, you will have some cover for your life-style until the 'rain' goes away. If you do not sacrifice now, you will sacrifice later, because it will rain. I teach folks to store, set aside, save for that storm, because it will come. When it comes, I want you to have sufficient 'rain gear' for those emergencies and/or unexpected/unwanted challenges that will happen in your life. I survived because I had the proper <u>garments</u> until the storm passed through my campground. This book will teach you how to do the same.

My third lesson:

Thou shall not use your credit card when you know that you will not have the money to pay the bill when the statement comes, especially when you don't need the items anyway.

I am always dumbfounded by how much a person can spend at some of their favorite stores (Kmart, Wal-Mart and Target) for items such as cleaning products, body care products, personal and necessity items to assist in their health and beauty care. The $1.99, $3.99 and $5.99 products can easily add up to about $100 per visit at the store and $500 for the month. I would go to the store as if I had great sums of money. I would purchase a cleaner for the kitchen sink, a cleaner for the kitchen counter, a cleaner for the toilet, a cleaner for the bathroom sink and a separate cleaner for the tub/shower. I even had different detergents for each family member. From my good credit days, I had a high credit limit on each of my credit cards; while unemployed, I used them as if I had unlimited funds to cover the charges once the bill arrived. Even though I would preach maintaining a budget, I did not want to accept that I needed a budget for those stores, especially on the important items that appear to be cheap. Because the items were cheap, I would buy in bulk; I figured I was saving. When I used my credit card in the past and I paid in full by the end of the month, the interest cost was zero. Now, I am paying interest from those credit card charges, items such as toothpaste, hand lotion and facial soap. Let me break it down: in January I bought toothpaste for $1.99, if unpaid that same 'paste' could cost around $2.19 not including tax in December. I hear you; you are saying that's not worth mentioning. Let's take your whole shopping cart of $500. How much do you think that would cost you? It would cost a whopping $90 in interest expense, if unpaid in 12 months. Is it worth it? I became more educated in my own experience. Always, have a budgeted list with you, even when you are shopping for items that do not cost much. I will tell you that when I went to the store with a credit card, I felt free to shop and buy just anything; shopping is what I enjoyed. I was good at it. I had to learn that you are not free when shopping with a credit card, because those charges are not free. I did not think about how I was going to pay the bill. Now, I understand the importance of carrying your budget everywhere you go. Yes, everywhere, even when you think you are only going to buy just one item. Something takes over our minds when we walk in the stores. I teach that when you first walk in the store, you need to pull out your budgeted list and a hand-held calculator. Also, I teach to be upfront and discuss with your family all of the absolute things that are truly needed, set your budget and never buy over what's on your list even if you have a credit card.

My fourth lesson:

Thou shall get rid of people and things
that are of no value in your life.

Dispose of all assets that bring you and/or your financial net-worth down. Also, 'trash' the stuff that does not add to your positive worth. Sometimes this is the hardest thing to do since we quickly fall in love with people and things that come into our galaxy. Okay, I will give you the benefit of the doubt. When we first obtain an item it appears to be great. It is working well, it looks good or we feel great when we are near it. But, do you remember what your elders have told you about objects in your life that take up space? YOU SHOULD CONDUCT A PERIODIC INVENTORY AND ASK THE FOLLOWING QUESTION: **Is there value in what you want and/or what you have?** Well, you should get rid of those (persons and/or things) that do not add some substance to your life. During my down period, I had a difficult time letting go of anything because at the time I felt as if I needed everything in my possession. I am speaking of stuff. I guess you are asking if I am still talking about finances. Yes, please remember and recognize that everything is financial. Your time is money, your effort is money, things take money and your money is your money. Everything and every second spent on one thing is an opportunity cost for something else to be possibly missed. Let me say it this way, by having one particular item may cause you to miss having another particular item. For example, if you have an old TV and you are still paying on it, you may feel obligated to keep it until you pay for the item in full. This may cause you to miss out on an opportunity to purchase a new TV at a discounted rate and within your budget. You are hooked on that old TV. Yet, it is not adding anything to your net-worth. It is bringing you down, because it is always broken and you still owe the creditor more than you care to remember. In this example, let's say that you owe close to $1,250 dollars. See calculation below for the net-worth of this particular asset:

Debt accumulated from television (TV)	$1,250	amount owed
Value of TV set	$ 750	asset's value
Net-Worth in asset	($ 500)	negative, less than zero

The TV is valued at $750, but your net-worth in that television set is negative $500. As shown above, to compute the net-worth you must deduct the debt from the value of your asset. The TV is calculated as such ($750-$1,250); you owe more than the asset is currently worth. Consequently, this asset is worthless – it's trash. Well, this is how I was with my stuff. It didn't matter if the stuff was worthless and had no financial value. I wanted it all, it was mine and I was very much attached to ALL of it. I am not telling you to replace all items that are old and have a negative worth. I am suggesting that you consider, **look at what you have and ask the question: is this asset adding something positive to your life?** I challenge you to think about this before you buy anything else. How much are you willing to put into the product that you are interested in purchasing? I plead that you think about the total interest costs you will be paying, the maintenance agreement fees and routine checkup costs. These fees add to the total cost of your purchase, all costs added over the product's life span. **Is the cost worth your time, energy and limited funding? This is my appeal; do not just look at the product without considering the total cost. Do it upfront (before the purchase) and update your inventory yearly (after the purchase).** Let me mention that taking inventory includes 'people' too. However, I will not discuss this category in this book. Also, taking inventory is not just for businesses but for individuals as well. I will discuss the details on taking inventory further into this book.

My fifth lesson:

Thou shall not watch or listen to depressing news
about the economy, the high unemployment rate or
the slim chance of you finding another job.

Remember if you have <u>HOPE</u>, it does not matter what is going on around you. You just look up, trust in the higher power and plan for your future. If you apply yourself, whether it is to find a job or whether it is to meet your basic needs – you will succeed when you believe. Since I am not a psychiatrist, I cannot force you to change through prescribed medicine or psychological treatments. However, I do teach that you must believe that you will survive whatever you are going through. If you hope for a million dollars and have a plan of action, you may not get that exact amount, but you may get close. I will not make any promises, but I will say that **attitude makes a difference**. Live sensibly and dream abundantly. Be prudent in your spending, but think bountifully in your personal objectives and aspirations. And, when people come to you to discuss that remote chance of getting hired or that fat chance of reaching those personal goals just change the subject. Try to obtain the information that is needed in a neutral way without the negative emotions and/or opinions. Sometimes, I just did not listen to the news at all. Some folks even laughed at me for not keeping up with the daily 'negative' rates and prices, but I am happy. I have HOPE, and no one can take that away from me, even when I was eliminated from employment. It was just like obtaining a college degree, once you get it, no one can take it away. Well, I have a degree in 'HOPE' and I hope that you can grab some of your own from this book to keep.

My sixth lesson:

Thou shall quit making excuses that you cannot follow
your dream(s) since you have no money.

I had it all planned out; I was working, making money and saving. I was packed with dreams that I wanted to reach. Consequently, on that bright and sunny day, I went to work to only learn our company was being downsized again. This time I was released from work. I was eliminated from the workforce. Are you asking, if I have given up? No, I did not give up even though my funds were limited and I had no paying job. With no job, I had the time to write, to conduct research analysis, process consumer surveys for my dream book and to market this book to grand folks like you. I teach individuals to use what they have. If time is what one has then use that. If energy is what one has then use that. I found out that I was able to use my 'time' and 'energy' without using my 'money' in which case, I had none. In this world, there are numerous ways to meet your dreams. There are more than the simple two ways: the direct and indirect way to accomplish your goals. There is a large spectrum of ways to meet your dreams and some of them may not take a large supply of money. Do you believe me? Well, test me and just try to prove me wrong. I challenge you to fulfill your dreams, but first read this book.

My seventh lesson:

Thou shall be grateful for what you have.

If you must dish out the funds, remember to only obtain the goods/services free and clear of long-term debt. Most of us have a bunch of stuff, yet we are still unhappy with what we have. Personally, I had to learn to enjoy my old stuff and look at those run down items differently. Please note that I am exaggerating; I was just use to replacing things sooner and not waiting until my goods broke down. Case-in-point, if the life span of a computer was three years, then I replaced my computer after two years. My household products' life would depend on what the government said the life of that particular product was to be. I had the current Internal Revenue Code, which states the life of every product there is out there except for a cell phone. And my cell phone was replaced yearly. I felt as if I was being tested. How could I be grateful with an old phone? Yes, it worked, but it was huge and it did not have the latest and greatest features on it. Here I am a financial consultant; I was conducting seminars at no cost and performing consultations at minimum cost. Yet I was having a difficult time using an old computer and an ancient cell phone. I had to practice what I was preaching. Once, I was back on track with my own teachings, I was able to look at things in my life that needed adjusting. I had a different perspective outside what the governmental agencies were saying in regards to my goods. Thank goodness I had this change of heart before I went out and bought new items with attached debt. Although my items were old, they were mine, free and clear of any long-term debt. This was my budget. I was happy and at peace to not have any debt (except for the house note).

Lastly, I enjoyed my products even during the storm because I was self-sufficient. I still have that self-sufficiency today. Allow me to teach you how to be self-sufficient and to get prepared before the storm, to endure during the storm, and to repair (fix-up) after the storm. Just remember to invite your family to stroll with you under that 'umbrella'. If you are the one holding the frame of the umbrella, let the family know your path so that the unit may glide together in and through the storm(s). Do not attempt to walk alone; be content with your family, and grateful for the goods that you have. Don't forget to gain and/or improve your financial insight by embracing the tools that are provided in this book. Enjoy.

My Finance Journey: starting Friday, 8 May 2009

This section represents the beginning of my real life experience on managing through 24 months of unemployment with a dependent. What is written here is the time log of my personal financial struggle from the start of the day I was released from the job. Although, it was very difficult at times, this was necessary because my unemployment added more insight to the inter-workings of the tools that I teach. I received a deeper knowledge on the practicality of the financial tools that I have provided in this book. This book written by the alphabet shows numerous in-depth ways on how to survive when you don't have enough funds to meet even the basic needs. I am here to tell you that my techniques work.

8:00 AM

God sent the Holy Spirit to my office, a Christian organization where I worked, to inform me that this was going to be my last day of employment with this organization. The Holy Spirit instructed me to clean up, to pack up because I was going to be let go…released…given the pink slip. I was instructed not to be angry, but to walk out with grace. Well, everything happened as God said it would. But looking back, I tried to understand why I did not believe the 'voice' that I was hearing. Did I think that this would never happen to me – a CPA, a person with a MBA? Did I believe the MAN, my boss, who tried to reassure me that he would never fire me while he was working there! I guess I thought I was considered a valued employee. By the way, I made a cash bank deposit earlier on this day. This morning, I was BOLDLY talking back to God. "There is obviously a mistake; someone else's name should be written on that separation notice." Did you not know that I am a child of God: I am born anew? I know that 'Numbers' is a book in the Old Testament. I go to church every Sunday and I have a favorite scripture. I trust the Lord with all my heart and I lean not to my own understanding. Yet, I wanted to understand.

4:00 PM

Now, I am getting assistance in packing up my stuff from HR and the boss MAN. I even got to take the office plant. Just think, two months ago I spoke at a workshop on the importance of saving and budgeting. I couldn't believe it. My dream was to teach individuals how to manage their money through saving and budgeting. **Here's my basic theory: you wouldn't leave home without your wallet, so why do you leave home without your budget. But first, you must follow your dreams…do you have any dreams?** These would be personal objectives that you want to accomplish before you…pass on to another place. This is what I was communicating to the workshop attendees; all the while, in my head I am praying to the Lord to help me (push me) to write a book. My dream is to share how the Lord has blessed me with parents and grandparents who taught me how not to let that 'almighty dollar' control me. My grandfather thought he had the 'key' to obtaining and increasing wealth of those all-powerful green paper bills. His wealth was through others who seem to disregard and/or throw away small change. At the expense of others, he was always spending time digging in other folks' couches to find any loose change. He had a way of convincing the folks that what he found now belonged to him. He never released any of his funds, not even that copper brown thing, worth no more than a **cent**. He was wise, yet to the extreme. My grandmother on the other hand believed in 'investing'. She would always have something to give to her prized investments - her grandchildren. My mother taught us about budgeting and after my father passed, we were still able to live comfortably and travel around the world through family budgeting without disposing it senselessly in the world.

Now, I teach individuals how to take the P from Penny and produce their own P-pot using my invention of the 4P-system. Being seasoned in the financial world through the ups and downs, **I have developed my own system called: value and price the Ps please. First you Pray – then Plan (budget), then Pay (bills) and finally you Play.** I guess, I forgot one major P, you need to get PAID.

As I was walking out to my unpaid new car with my walking papers, my thoughts were that I was sure going to miss that 'P' and I am not talking about those 'peas' from the pot. I am talking about getting PAID. Would I still PRAY? Not to mention – Planning for the future - Paying those bills – Playing with my child. We all must 'play' sometimes, but on the

8th of May, my path was being redirected again. It appears that I am starting over again, a new beginning with personal struggles. I needed to personally learn how to endure with the high prices in the current market as an unemployed single parent. God wanted me to fully understand what others have gone through and what others are currently going through financially. With this new knowledge base, I am better able to educate others on how to PRESS forward and keep the FAITH even though you cannot see what's ahead. I am learning how to allow God to direct my path.

Please allow me to teach you how to season (set up) your Ps, slowly process your Ps and enjoy your Ps, even when you feel you are lacking or missing the main 'Pea' from the pot. Let's continue to pray by asking the Lord to show you how to manage even when there is only one P left in the pot.

Introduction

How does money grow in your household?

Did you know that money grows in your household? Money grows by the income that you earn, the government assistance you obtain, the child support funds you receive and/or sometimes income from that hobby you enjoy. But the question is what happens with the money once it has matured (been received) in your household? Do you show it off and let everyone know how much you have or do you kick it out as soon as you have obtained the funds? When I say kick it out, I mean, you spend it at the first opportunity you get and you don't care if you need the item(s) or not? You just cannot keep it. Have you heard the saying that some people can't hold water? Well some people can't hold money! It is almost like you are allergic to it. Maybe you get sick when you get some money. You break out in hives and you don't allow 48 hours to pass, a sale to pass or even that urge to pass before you are racing to buy something because you feel that you have the right to have the item(s). You have even convinced yourself that God has communicated to you to buy it. Now you want to get rid of that itch. Therefore, you head to the store or turn on the computer and boom: the purchase is made. A year later, you ask yourself, what happened to my baby? The money is gone. You are older now and you do not have the strength or energy to plant the money, reproduce the money into something more or bigger. Now, that $1.00 bill is worthless; the weeds from inflation have taken over. You have nothing to show for the work you have done over the years. It's gone, gone, and gone. Is this you? If so, then there may be hope if you are willing to follow the steps in this book. You will need to clip off the dead stems and replant the seed money. Don't forget to fertilize even if it's as small as a mustard seed, water it on a regular basis and let it grow. This book will show you how. Are you willing and able?

Is it real or play money?

Now, I realize that you are working hard to live the life style of the rich and famous. But, are you working with 'real' money or 'play' money? Is the money that you are spending free and clear of any charges such as interest, penalties or late fees? Is the cash-on-hand your asset or your debt? Sometimes, we play games with others and our aim is to purchase 'Board Walk', but before we get there we don't even have $200 to purchase that asset. So, we walk to the bank or to the fast cash agency and turn over maybe the only asset that we have to get some play money that is only obtainable through towering fees. When I say play money, I am talking about money that is not our asset, but we want it in order to live the 'board walk' lifestyle. We are playing monopoly with money that is loaned to us to beat out the opponent. We are given credit that we turn into our 'play' money. We are allowed to use the creditor's money for a brief time. We want the funds to entertain our associates, to impress our neighbor or to have it at our leisure. Now, how long do you go around before you yell out that you do not want to 'play' anymore? Is the game over when you do not have any more money? What about the fees? Are you able to pack them up and place them in the box until the next time you play the game? What happens when you do not make your monthly payments from the previous month's play-time? Are the creditors keeping you from playing again and keeping you from getting even more play money? If this is you, then put down that board game and read on. Learn a new game and only move forward with real money. As you move across the 'board game' with infrequent money deposits around the board called life, don't end up being a prisoner of bad credit, constantly borrowing money or playing a life style above your means. Stop playing with money that is not yours and money that comes with a high price; play only with the 'real' thing.

Do you have a license to spend?

Did you know that you need a license to spend? Yes, you need a license stating that you have a legal authorization to spend money. Have you taken a test on the skills of spending? (See Appendix: The Spending ID Card with instructions and Chapter Q) You are probably asking, who would have the authority to provide me with a 'spending' license? Well, who has given you the right to spend all of your money, anyway? Have you registered the money assigning you as 'legal guardian?' Were you given official permission to spend freely? Don't put down this book until you have answered the questions. Have you been given the exclusive and excessive freedom, with no restraints and full clearance, to spend all of your earned money and/or borrowed money? Didn't your elders tell you that there are rules to the 'act of spending?' After reading this book, you will be able to obtain your learner's permit; but to obtain your full dispensation license, you must take the exam twice a year, pass it and carry it wherever you go. Please note that you could go to the 'I have no money left to spend' jail, if you do not follow the rules stated on your license. The first exam is taken as soon as you have finished the book and the second exam is taken six months later. Before you take the exam, study your habits, recognize your dire need to spend and realize a change is necessary. You can grade your own exam; you will pass the test with some given stipulations. Please do not look for the answers; the answers are in your head. The test is used as an instrument to help you document what rules and/or practices you must follow to understand your **spending ABCs (attitudes, behaviors and characteristics)**. Once you have read this book and have taken the exam, you will understand very well the basic terms budgeting, setting allowances and how to stay above water. As you are reading, it will become clear the tools that you must carry with you daily. Also, you will recognize the importance of not leaving home without your spending license. Metaphorically speaking, you will learn how to drive the given speed limit with sufficient 'air' while maintaining a 'spare' for emergencies. Throughout this book, you will gain insight to your personal spending 'pressure' gage and you will learn how not to overspend.

Do you prefer premium or regular?

When I first purchased my car, I specifically remember the salesman telling me to ONLY use *regular* gasoline in my gas tank. It was clear by my facial expression that I was puzzled, so I mumbled to myself. Why did he have to insult me like that? I had just purchased Toyota's top of the line, and now I wanted to know how he could demand me to purchase just *regular* gas. Didn't he think that my brand new baby (I mean Toyota) deserved better than that? How would it look to drive up into a gas station and purchasing *regular*? After spending hundreds of dollars to clean out the *premium* residue stuck in my tank, I wish I had listened to the salesman in the beginning. Although, I was still puzzled; I had to question myself, why was it necessary for me to buy *premium* anyway? Here's another example. I saw this skirt that I adored, but it did not have a well-known brand name attached to it. First, I questioned myself, how often would someone peel at the back of a skirt to see the brand name? Well, it was the principle of the matter! I hadn't accepted that I could feel pretty with this 'no name brand' skirt. I battled whether I could be happy with it on in public. However, I did make the purchase; let's call it the *regular* skirt. It was not a *premium*, top of the line, doubled stitched but it was cheap. Every time I wore that *regular* skirt, I would get compliments. My response was, "thank you, but I must tell you that this *regular* skirt's brand name is not well-known." Even though, I liked this *regular* skirt, I did not feel *premium* when I wore it out. Now, are your purchases *regular* or *premium*? **Do your purchases determine who you are?** Do you only feel *premium* when you have *premium* stuff? I use to work at a bank and I met a great deal of *premium* folks with a whole lot of *premium* money, yet they were still unhappy. In this book, I will discuss being content in your own class. I will discuss the options and when it is appropriate to only purchase *premium* and when it is necessary to purchase *regular*. **Remember, once you recognize your ABCs and realize your purpose, you will not need material things to complete you. Your dreams, goals and aspirations, currently in your head, once accomplished will complete you.** Once you learn to write down your goals, your focus will no longer be on 'stuff'; you will be satisfied with the progress towards your purpose. Now, I am proud of my 'stuff' and I am no longer embarrassed. When someone compliments me on my *regular* purchases, I say, "thank you."

Is your plate too full?

On this earth, we have so much to choose from and sometimes it is difficult to say NO. It is tough to say, I have had enough for the moment. So, we continue to add and add and add until the stuff on our plate overflows and falls off. Do you feel that since you have a plate that it is okay to fill it up? So what if it overflows? Does it meet your approval, if you received your money's worth? Well, I need to inform you that your money's worth today may not be enough for you tomorrow. You see your appetite for 'stuff' gets bigger and bigger and bigger. Now you want MORE and MORE and MORE. You no longer can be satisfied with just ONE over stuffed plate. Even though your income has not changed, you are not happy or even content with just ONE; you are always going to want MORE. So now I ask, did you really need all of that? Could you be happy with five pairs of BLACK shoes or do you feel the need for 15 pairs? Are there 15 shades of BLACK? Do you really need a house with five full bathrooms when there are only three people in your family? Is it necessary to have a car for Church, a car for Work and a car for Play? Now, I will ask again, "Is your plate too full?" While reading the book, you will be asked to list your inventory, apply an age and value to each item. Mark each item with the colors GREEN, YELLOW and/or RED pen or highlighter. Follow the instructions in the book as to what to do with the RED marked items before you add anything else to your plate. Do not be afraid to do this; you will not become malnourished once you get rid of the RED items. Trust that once you become happy with less, your need for an overloaded plate will become less gratifying. And, if you do find a need to have more, go back for 'seconds' later. Wait for at least 48 hours, and then ask yourself, do I still have a need for this item? If yes, then get another plate and have at it. If no, then move on to something else. Let's discuss, what if they run out of the item after you have waited the allotted time? What should you do now? It will be okay. You will manage without that item. Just say to the ultimate buyer, this is your time and opportunity to 'stuff yourself' with the item. Either you will pay for it now or you will pay for it later. After reading this book and following the guidelines, you will learn how to not look at your neighbor's plate but to focus on your own plate. And, if you follow the instructions noted in this book, your appetite will diminish; you will finally realize that there is more room for the more important things in your life.

Just manage that one dollar for now!

I have conducted numerous interviews: some while in college as a team member on a project, some at companies as a volunteer and some at shopping malls as a concerned party (but extremely curious!). Here is what I have learned. Your spending habits will stick with you wherever you go. It doesn't matter if you make $10.00 per hour or $10,000 per month. If you spend loosely with very little income, you will most definitely spend loosely with huge sums of money. Mark my word if you are poor and unhappy with less than $1,000 in the bank, then you will be poor and unhappy with a $1,000,000. Why? This is because you won't be able to hold onto that new money. You'll have it just for a moment. You will find ways to spend all of your money. And before you know it, you will be poor again. Of course, not everybody will conduct their money matters this way, just the ones with the bad spending habits. The bad habits mean that you do not have a written budget for you to review regularly. You do not have a plan, long-term goals that are written, followed and updated as necessary. You have family, friends, neighbors, store owners and creditors who control you and/or your money. You dream daily of having at least $1 million dollars and how this will change your life. **Your focus has been on how to obtain the money** instead of focusing on what you would do with the money once you get it in your hands. Case-in-point, what did you do with that unexpected check, that monetary gift you received last year, that inheritance, that refund check and/or that bonus? Do you have a written plan regarding extra funds that come across your path? What is the first thing that you do when you get paid? Be honest - what are your spending habits? Do you know your ABCs: (attitudes, behaviors and characteristics) regarding money? What are you weak for? What are the items that you must have at all cost? I am not trying to crush your main dream of obtaining a large sum of money dropping at your front door step. I just want you to dream about your plans before you obtain the money. Also, to reach your goals, you would need to document how you plan to reach that goal at a smooth steady pace, patience and perseverance. Add these words to the Ps mentioned in the P chapter: Pace, Patience, and Perseverance. The terms will assist you in staying focused on your goals and not giving up on them. This is not a **get rich fast** scheme. But similar to a tortoise, moving forward at a steady pace mixed with a PLAN is the direction that you must take. After you have completed this book, challenge yourself to set a plan of action so that you can press forward on your long life purpose(s) allowing the cash to be a byproduct to get you there. Focus first on understanding your spending habits, and then change them for the better. And, when you come across some extra funds you will know exactly what to do with it. Remember, if you can manage one dollar well, you will be given an opportunity to manage twice that amount then seven times that amount and so on... With a steady pace, you will manage that as well. For now, you should just start with that \$1.00. This book will show you how to become an effective manager with the money you have by teaching you how to be independently free and to increase wealth from where you are one step at a time.

What about the kids?

Mommy/Daddy, why are we so poor? Do not say that you are poor because you have a child or children. Actually you are 'rich' with kids in your life. You get all sorts of deductions and tax credits because of them. You are head of the household or married with exemptions because of them. You are even able to get health and car insurance cheaper because of them. The insurance companies think you are stable, so you get special deductions.

People, in general, soften up when they see you have kids. Family cars are less expensive than sports cars. So how can you say you are poorer because of the kids? The children can make things happen at a reduced rate for you. What a shame that we live in a world where we know the cost of everything but the value of nothing. We do not realize nor recognize the value we have in our dependents. Take the time out and discuss the kids. Now that we have them, we ought to care for them because they are our precious cargo; their value is 'priceless.' The value is so high that they are considered an off-balance sheet asset item. Yet, they add to our net-worth.

Parents, I need you to take responsibility and change those bad habits. You must break the curse. Look behind you and/or below, there is someone watching you. Stop! It is necessary to make the change before you have NO change to ex-change. In this book, you will obtain the tools to teach your kids how to manage, for starters, with very small change. You may need to start from scratch by teaching the A-B-Cs to your dependents. Your babies need to take baby steps up the ladder by starting with A Budgeted Cashbook. They cannot move off their baby formula until you as the parent are comfortable with your own solid food. Once they see you chewing your food properly and not taking big chunks of food before swallowing, then you may increase the family's diet. You must not add to the alphabet soup until you have managed that 'pure milk' – CASH. You cannot eat Cereal (credit cards) and more Dessert (debit cards) until you have mastered the basic formula milk. Now, as you are relearning how to eat (spend) properly again, don't forget your kids are watching and learning from you. Realize that they are watching because they need you to **succeed and not fail**. So, stop getting heartburn and start setting a good example. Read this book, slow down and enjoy your meal (money).

Yes, I do understand it is difficult to change one's ways, but it's possible to make a break through. Of course, it is easier to develop yourself before the mold is set. Just remember that all things are possible when you recognize where your strength comes from. Accordingly, get charged up to make that change. Here is a brief lesson on how to get off baby food and to walk independently.

a. Write-down how long the meal ($money) must last. See appendix: Cash Calendar.
b. Budget the amount you want to digest in one sitting.
c. Pick from a variety of seasonings and sauces; slow cook the meal. Take the time out and develop a financial plan.
d. Taste and chew the food before the final swallow (analyze before making the purchase).
e. Don't over stuff your plate. Take very small bites.
f. Savor (enjoy your purchase) every item on the plate.
g. Don't eat all of the food (funds) in one sitting.
h. Save some for a rainy day or when you are unable to dine out!!

In this book, the letters of the alphabet (ABCs) denoted in the chapters are used to guide you, as the reader, toward smart and purposeful spending while planning for the future. There are numerous tools established in this book to help you and your family through your personal journey to financial independence. You along with your household members will be empowered to use the fun-filled techniques to the quest of building financial success and wealth.

CHAPTER ABC –
Attitudes, Behaviors and Characteristics

Before you jump in and work on that budget with an effort to manage your family's total income and expenses, you first need to understand your spending habits. It is very difficult to change your habits without recognizing your wants and needs in life. Your spending habits tell you and everyone around you what's important to you. Your heart is where your money is. This is a good time to understand why you must have what you must have. Sometimes when I have a stressful week, I have that urge to buy something special and it does not matter if I have the money or not. I will go to the store and pick up the first outfit that can make me smile and/or make me forget about my troubles. To avoid giving in to my weakness for a cute outfit, especially when I had a bad week, I developed an alternative plan by going somewhere that is cheap, safe and fun to relieve the stress. Also, I would consider doing something that will at least in my mind release the tension. I would set aside available things to do just in case I have an unpleasant week. The list may include, but doesn't have to be limited to the following:

- Going to a funny and entertaining movie
- Walking in the park while enjoying the scenery
- Dancing to some music in the living-room
- Soaking in the tub with sweet smelling candles

Now, I suggest that you come up with a ready-made list of things to do in place of going to the store to spend money on items that you do not have a need for and do not have the money to buy. Before you develop that list, you must first recognize what makes you spend more than the funds you have. What makes you spend money over and above the bare necessities? Start with that big house and/or that expensive car; meditate on why you have all that stuff. Is there a need that was not met when you were a child? What makes you spend more than the funds you have available to you? There was a time when I would purchase expensive cars because I was convinced the cost was linked to safety. I thought an expensive car was costly because the manufacturer used expensive parts so that the car would never malfunction. And, I thought expensive parts would never need to be fixed. Well, with time, I recognized that expensive cars also break down and the parts were expensive to replace. So, instead of buying an expensive car over and above what my household could manage at the time, I obtained a 24-hour automobile service for unexpected breakdowns. Now, when my car breaks down, I just call the 1-800 service number and they will either tow my car or jump start it so that I can get to my destination safe and sound. Buying a 49.99 yearly tow service was cheaper than spending an extra $49,999 on a car that would still break down. Now, I want you and everyone in your family to sit down and discuss every major item in your possession. For example, discuss:

1. Why did you pay $850 for a microwave, when you could have purchased an adequate one for $150?
2. Why do you have 50 pair of shoes, more than the number of days in a month? Is it necessary to have 4 cars when there are only 2 drivers in the household?
3. Why do you go to the store to buy one item, yet you leave the store with several shopping bags totaling to more than $275?

Everyone must crawl before they walk; therefore, you must know your ABCs (that is your **a**ttitude, **b**ehavior and **c**haracteristics) before you complete the remaining alphabet chapters related to financial planning. It is imperative that you must take the time out of your busy spending schedule and analyze your spending habits. No one can conduct this better than you. This adventure is not necessarily to share with others, but to understand your makeup in the area of spending. This is your starting point to improve your financial management.

SUB-CHAPTER A:
Analyze your family's lifestyle!

The "A" represents, alpha, the beginning of your life in regards to spending. Analyzing your family's lifestyle is the start of good financial management. You have purchased this book to launch or rebirth your efforts toward money management. It is my intent to guide you through this book by using the letters of the alphabet to simplify the process. The aim is not to tell you what to do with your money; I just want you to analyze what makes you spend the way that you do. Once you recognize what makes you spend and why you spend, then you (and only you) can change those ways. If this is your desire, you can move forward, once you realize what triggers you to purchase those goods and services.

Here are the things that could trigger you to make certain purchases:

a. Your hunger and thirsts for an item
b. Your children making their desires known (with those sad faces)
c. Your mood (physical & mental)
d. Your environment (status symbol)
e. Your education/background
f. Your upbringing

Below are some additional influences that may have an effect on you making that purchase:

a. TV/Radio commercials
b. Newspaper sales and ads
c. Neighbors and/or work acquaintances
d. Family and/or friends
e. Internet pop-ups and emails
f. At leisure shopping

Take the time out upfront to analyze your family's spending habits. If you know your triggers, then you can control them…use them to your benefit. For example, my weakness is my daughter yelling out her desires in the store and telling me how she will be teased by her classmates if I do not purchase those items for her. Since I recognize that I most likely will appease her, even though I know that she does not need that item, I tend to shop without her. Also, I cannot window shop without spending some money. Generally, when I shop leisurely, I am bored. When I am bored, I see things (lots of things) that I want and because I am leisurely shopping – I buy just about anything that appears to be cheap and I buy everything that I see and like. I cannot leisurely shop, ever. Whenever, I have extra time on my hands, I will go to the movies and buy popcorn (if it is within the budget) or do a puzzle. And, when I am forced to go to the mall, I keep a puzzle that I will enjoy completing while everyone else is shopping. I have recognized my spending habits and triggers, now I strongly recommend that your family unit individually analyze, acknowledge and accept their own spending practices. Encourage and groom your family to change to a new and improved spending style that is pleasing for the whole family.

To analyze your family's spending life style you must document your daily spending. This is performed on each item spent from dawn to dust, which includes all internet shopping to personal store visits, from low-cost (bubble gum) items to high-ticketed items. I recommend conducting this project for at least a month to three months if you have the energy. Also, document the triggers that encouraged you to make that purchase.

Use this list to get you started: (add lines as needed)

Day X: Purchase 1: clothing, evening-wear. Trigger: at leisure shopping (nothing else to do).

Day 1: Purchase #1: ____________ Trigger: ________ Cost:__________
Purchase #2: ____________ Trigger: ________ Cost:__________
Purchase #3: ____________ Trigger: ________ Cost:__________
Purchase #4: ____________ Trigger: ________ Cost:__________
Day 2: Purchase #1: ____________ Trigger: ________ Cost:__________
Purchase #2: ____________ Trigger: ________ Cost:__________
Purchase #3: ____________ Trigger: ________ Cost:__________
Purchase #4: ____________ Trigger: ________ Cost:__________
Day 3: Purchase #1: ____________ Trigger: ________ Cost:__________
Purchase #2: ____________ Trigger: ________ Cost:__________
Purchase #3: ____________ Trigger: ________ Cost:__________
Purchase #4: ____________ Trigger: ________ Cost:__________

Day 4: Purchase #1: ____________ Trigger: ________ Cost:__________
Purchase #2: ____________ Trigger: ________ Cost:__________
Purchase #3: ____________ Trigger: ________ Cost:__________
Purchase #4: ____________ Trigger: ________ Cost:__________
Day 5: Purchase #1: ____________ Trigger: ________ Cost:__________
Purchase #2: ____________ Trigger: ________ Cost:__________
Purchase #3: ____________ Trigger: ________ Cost:__________
Purchase #4: ____________ Trigger: ________ Cost:__________
Day 6: Purchase #1: ____________ Trigger: ________ Cost:__________
Purchase #2: ____________ Trigger: ________ Cost:__________
Purchase #3: ____________ Trigger: ________ Cost:__________
Purchase #4: ____________ Trigger: ________ Cost:__________
Day 7: Purchase #1: ____________ Trigger: ________ Cost:__________
Purchase #2: ____________ Trigger: ________ Cost:__________
Purchase #3: ____________ Trigger: ________ Cost:__________
Purchase #4: ____________ Trigger: ________ Cost:__________

Table 1: Document your triggers

Now that you have finally figured out how you spend your money. The next step is to figure out what you spend your money on. There are three simple categories:

a. High ticketed items
b. Multiple low cost items
c. Both – just spend money

If you know "what" you spend your money on, then you can hone in on your "shopping behaviors" and sharpen your skills on how to manage your finances. To improve the way you spend, you must answer these five pertinent questions:

1. How do you spend money?
2. What do you spend money on?
3. Where do you spend the most money?
4. When do you spend a significant amount of your money?
5. Why do you spend money?

Based on prior analysis, there are individuals that are enjoying life too much and care nothing about their future. Are you that person? Have you considered how you are going to pay your mortgage or rent if you are laid off from your job next year? Have you thought about retirement, death or other long-term concerns? Honestly, do you care whether or not you leave your loved ones in debt? These questions explain your ABCs towards money, spending and financial management. The "A" for attitude, the "B" for behavior and the "C" for characteristics - explain how you manage your routine expenses. Whether you have a penny or a million dollars your ABCs personalized framework is the same. Whether you just got paid or you are low on funds, your ABCs will show off and show out in the same matter. So, if you spend money as if there is no tomorrow, with no "cents" then you will spend money as if there is no tomorrow, with a million "cents". Remember, your no non-sense spending will follow you until you are able to make some "sense" on how you spend, re-learn your ABCs and channel your family for a change. Therefore, before you inherit that million, I recommend that you obtain the necessary tools to learning the financial alphabet and perfect it with constant practice through budgeting.

Here are the definitions that may help you understand how and why you spend the way you do.

Attitude is a complex mental state involving beliefs and feelings and values and dispositions to act in certain ways. For example, "he has the attitude that spending money is fun." Your attitude on spending is usually based on your upbringing.

Behavior is the action or reaction of something (the substance is money) under specified circumstances. For example, "the behavior of XYZ family is studied by their spending actions; give them some money and watch how they spend it." I cannot go to the store when I am hungry; I just cannot think clearly when I have not eaten in awhile. Sometimes I will end up buying more things in haste to get out of the store to eat.

Characteristics is the integer part (positive or negative) of the representation when confronted with money; typical or distinctive (quality). For example, his character is to spend in order to obtain whatever he wants and it does not matter whether or not he has the funds. This gentleman's character is to impress those who may cross his path. He has a top model car with a distinctive suit on in order to come across first-class. You cannot tell on the outside that he is penny-less; he looks good with all of his treasures. His character shows that he is worth something by his possessions. Here's another example, a guy's character is to spend only if the item is in the budget. This is the best way to be, to only spend when the expense has been considered in advance and you can afford the purchase at that particular time. My character is to spend when someone does something special for me or I am pleased with their actions. For example, when my daughter makes good grades I tend to take her out to eat at her favorite restaurant. My character says to spend money on her even when I do not have the money to do such a kind gesture. I want to give back for her excellent conduct in school. My character is to treat people with a "good meal" when I feel good about them. This is my way to show appreciation to them. If I could treat all of my family, friends or anyone that has had a positive effect on me, I would definitely do so at a first-class rate. I cannot do this for everyone I come in contact with; therefore, I must set up a budgeted line-item called 'appreciation - dinner out.' What I do is look back at my previous month's experiences and I recognize those special folks to a grand meal that is strictly within my budget. Always remember that when you spend more in one expense category, then you must spend less in another category in order to meet the budget in total.

SUB-CHAPTER B:
Diminish buying, begging, biting and borrowing

There are four Bs your family should diminish: buying, begging, biting and borrowing. This section will break down the Bs for you here:

1. Stop BUYING stuff that you do not need.
2. Stop BEGGING for free money – nothing is free.
3. Stop BITING more than you can chew – spending more than the cash on hand.
4. Stop BORROWING and getting deeper into debt.

Let's start with the first B: stop buying stuff. This section is to understand why you buy stuff you don't need. Of course, it is nice to be able to buy special things with your money, especially since you worked hard for your money and you sacrificed free time from the family to make the money. But, is it necessary to beg, bite and borrow to BUY the things that you want? Most Americans are constantly buying things to make themselves happy. We are trying to fulfill that gap, yet we are not able to pay-off the items that we have already. It is okay to buy; I just recommend that the family members set limits on spending. Implement a budget plan and set aside discretionary funds in order to buy stuff that you really would like to have and/or need. In essence, only buy stuff that is within your budgeting guidelines. When you are willing to diminish the BEES of buying, then you will reduce the chances of being stung by the "Buying Blues".

On to the second B: stop begging for free money. Please recognize that nothing is free. Sometimes you need to consider why you need the money anyway. Is the need urgent or do you not want to use your own money to satisfy your desire? Why not try to use your "free" card for when you really, I mean really need the money? There are folks that aim to get money for anything they want, such as begging to be able to go to a basketball game or to see a special production show. Some will even obtain funds to get a professional pedicure when the utilities have not been paid. Is that you? What happens when you really need the money? Would you have run out of resources to obtaining the money free? Also, remember that nothing is free. You need to think about what will you have to do in return or what will you have to give up in order to get the money. The general rule is to ask yourself if the person(s) were not available to give you the funds, would it be worth begging for the funds to make that purchase. Is it a want or a need? When you are willing to diminish the BEES of begging, then you will reduce the chances of being stung by the "Begging Blues".

Now, let's talk about the third B: stop BITING more than you can chew. Are you going to the store with a credit card or checkbook to make a purchase when you do not have the money to pay? When the credit card statement arrives, you do not have the funds to pay the bill in full. Sometimes you do not even have the "minimum" payment. Also, when the check is received by your bank, you do not even have sufficient funds to cover the check amount. Oh, what a shame! You are BITING too much and do not have the "teeth" to chop down the substance that you have purchased. Now, you are filling up with bad stuff that you cannot digest. You cannot process the stuff, and it gets worst. You have excess charges, fees and interest costs that will add to your bad debt and credit rating. Here's the solution. Only buy what is absolutely necessary. Other than a house and car, if you cannot pay the balance with 90 days (free of any interest fees), then I would question – do you really need the item!! When you are willing to diminish the BEES of biting, then you will reduce the chances of being stung by the "Biting Blues".

Finally, the fourth B is sometimes the hardest to diminish: stop borrowing. Sometimes, we fall into a deep trap. We buy, we beg, we bite and now to get up and out of a bad situation, we must borrow. Borrowing is similar to digging a ditch from down below. As you are digging the dirt out of the way, where are you shoveling the dirt? Are you getting deeper and deeper with no way out? You are probably borrowing because you want to buy something you feel you need. You are borrowing because you have begged for too much, now the person wants his/her money back so now you have to borrow to pay him/her back. You are borrowing because you have bit off too much and now you have to pay back with interest.

How do you stop doing something? First you start by <u>slowing down gradually</u> and then slowly come to a complete stop. Turn off the vehicle of borrowing; eliminate the opportunity to borrow unless it is absolutely necessary. Continue to pay-off all of the previous debt, starting with the debt with the highest interest rate and loan amount. Slow down the process of borrowing new funds. Ask yourself the question: can the family survive without the item? If this is the case, then do not borrow. Now, when you are willing to diminish the BEES of borrowing, then you will reduce the chances of being stung by the "Borrowing Blues".

SUB-CHAPTER C:
Obtain Cash, Credit and Capital

Let's think about the gears in a car. When one is low on lubricant, the oil from the other gears may be sufficient enough to keep the engine operating smoothly and freely. As you know by now, I am not talking about the gears in a car. I am speaking of the 3-Big Cs: Cash, Credit or Capital. These are the "gears" that you need financially. When one is running low, you can survive off of the other two Cs. You do not need "cash only" to survive. You need to have two out of the three Cs. So, when you have high valued capital and you need cash, you can manage by living off the equity from your capital. The best example of capital is your home. When you have great credit and you need cash, you can manage by living off a line of credit (LOC) for a short time period. Of course, the better of the three is "CASH", but there will be times when you need some cash and you have NONE; the other gears can push you through those difficult times until you are able to revamp your cash with a fresh new coat of lubricant for your main gear – CASH. Always remember to drive slowly just in case the other gears are not sharp enough to move the engine freely during rough times.

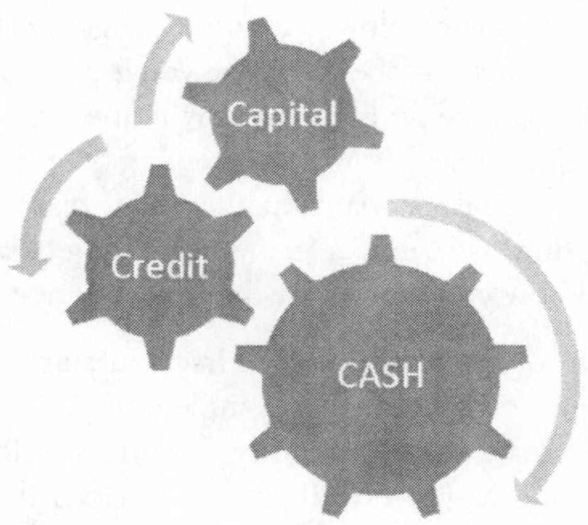

Process 1: The 3 Cs

When you have cash, this would be the time to set aside funds for a rainy day. I recommend setting aside three to six months' worth of your income. If you can do more, this would be great. Just do what you can; one step at a time. You never know when you will need it, and it is good to have. Even if you never lose your job, keep some cash stash away in a separate bank account. You may have a job where it has been a while since you have seen a salary increase, but gas prices, housing, food and other expenses are constantly going up. Maintain your 3-Cs security level by performing the following:

C-Cash	keep extra in a separate account(s) for urgent matters
C-Credit	pay bills timely for high credit ratings
C-Capital	obtain capital that increases in value

CHAPTER D –
How money is delivered!

Nowadays, there are multiple ways to receive your pay. There is the direct deposit, a live check, a debit card and of course, the old fashioned way – cash. How do you get paid? Sometimes when I get a physical check, I prefer it to be mailed and other times I want it to be handed over to me. I am even picky on how it is delivered. My preference is for the check to be sealed in a window envelope. I want to make sure that I am getting my own check and not someone else's check. Also, I want to ensure that no one is able to see the net amount and the deductions on my check. Once you get the check, the next thing to consider is what to do with the check. Do you cash it right away or do you deposit it into the bank? It is good to know exactly what will be done to the check before you get it in your hands. Do you divide the funds from the payroll check between your checking account and savings account? Do you get paid by the futuristic means of a "plastic" card? How are you able to use the card without any additional cost? I recommend understanding the details before using the card. For example does the card have an expiration date? Are you aware of additional cost that is attached to using the card? Do you have the option of setting up direct deposit? Or, do you go to a convenience store to cash your check and possibly spend the funds right there on the spot? Explain how you came to terms with the system that you use. This is the D chapter – how is your money delivered to you and how do you dish it out.

If you are the type of person that gets weak when money comes into the palm of your hands, then you want to obtain the funds without the direct contact of the money physically. Therefore, if your company has direct deposit then I suggest that you use that process. If your company does not have direct deposit and you cannot keep money for long, then you can take advantage of several other options, but first you must open up a bank account. If you cannot control how the money is delivered, then you must control how the money is "dished" out.

Here are some ways to control your funds without touching the cash:

- ✓ Direct Deposit
- ✓ Sign check....for deposit only.....deposit directly into your checking account
- ✓ Transfer via Internet a small percentage amount to go into the savings account.
- ✓ Prepare in advance a deposit slip for the expected cash....go directly to the bank (do not pass go).
- ✓ Write in "cash out" amount only if it has been budgeted.
- ✓ Do not carry a significant amount of cash (greater than $100) without having a documented plan where the money will be dished out.
- ✓ Do not cash the check at a convenience store or a place where you may be attempted to make a purchase. Those purchases are called "convenient". The store is there to make things <u>convenient</u> for you so that you will make purchases for your convenience. You may feel obligated because you feel that they have helped you by cashing your check. Now you want to help them by making a purchase. This is your subconscious working against you. Don't do it.

The bottom line is that you ought to control your cash at all times. If you want to buy something, then you buy when you are ready and not a minute sooner. Do not feel obligated to buy because you received the store's weekly sales paper and/or coupons to purchase products at a discount. I would suggest that you save the coupon and use it when the time is right for you to make that purchase. Do not feel duty-bound to "dish-out" the cash until the terms are precisely what you are willing to agree upon given that the items are pre-approved and documented in your budget. Therefore, if it's in the budget AND you can afford it AND the timing is on target with the family's personal objectives, then and only then, you can move forward and make that purchase.

Let's talk about the three (3) types of expenses for which people tend to dish out funds:

1. Fixed and/or required
2. Variable and/or discretionary
3. Luxury expenses

If the expense is fixed and/or required, then you probably have already signed a mutual agreement stating the complete terms and payment conditions. Once the agreement is signed, the payment terms are usually fixed set in stone and will not change until the full payment has been received. If special arrangements are made further into the contract, then a new agreement is signed and a new "settlement" is made. Nevertheless, in each stage of the game an agreement is signed and the dishing out of cash is based on those terms.

If the expense is variable and/or discretionary, then the payment is based on the services used or purchases made. In addition to the amount of services provided, you probably agreed to pay based of the services used during a period noted in the contract. Here you are able to increase/decrease the services provided to you at any given time, but the payment terms remain the same. For example, you may have been asked to pay by the 15th of each month for the services provided in the previous month. Also, the agreement may state that the company will only accept automatic transactions pulled from your checking account. Notice that the payment terms are fixed, even though the services are variable.

For the luxury items, I do not need to explain how you are triggered to buy these items because I do not know what turns you on to buy. Yet, I will advise you that these items still need to be placed in the budget and approved by the family members. You still need complete control on how your funds are dished out and delivered to pay for that "luxury". Even though, the item is your luxury, the payment terms must be based on what you can afford and handle given your current circumstances. Do not go deeper into debt by any luxury item, because the luxury will not make you feel better when it is time to make that payment.

It is important that you implement a procedure on how the cash will be delivered and dished out so that your family can maximize the funds the way they so desire. Think also in terms of the risk involved in obtaining the funds one way versus another way. If you obtain a debit card and you lose it, will it be replaced or is it lost forever. Think about the benefits and cost of the various ways of receiving your money. If you cannot control how the funds flow in, then control how the funds flow out. Plan ahead how the allocation of funds will occur. Remember spend time on the "details". The more time you spend up front on the details of how the cash will be handled, the more control you will have over the cash each pay period.

As this is the D-Chapter, it seems appropriate to discuss DEBT at this point in the book. Feel free to go to the website, www.ABCsthatmakecents.com, to obtain extra copies of the worksheets or turn to the Appendix (noted as the 4-1-1 schedules) and review the following:

Step 4	My Personal Payoff Contract	High level schedule
Step 11	Debt Schedule	Detailed-level schedule

Here is the 4-1-1 to debt repayment quick guide to regaining a full sense of control over your money:

- ✓ Recognize that repayment takes time and patience; never, ever give up
- ✓ Realize that with determination, there are many solutions
- ✓ Contact each creditor; inform them of the goal to pay-off your debt
- ✓ Keep your promise by religiously making those timely payments
- ✓ Continue to track your daily spending
- ✓ Make a commitment and do not incur any more debt
- ✓ Extra funds received should go toward paying down your debt
- ✓ Try to avoid bankruptcy and persist with your personal goal to pay-off the debt
- ✓ Pay off debt with fortitude and precision; set up a method and follow through
- ✓ Don't allow the creditors to force you to pay more than you are able to; stay on track with your personal plan
- ✓ Recalculate your budget, each time a creditor's balance is eliminated; increase your payment to another creditor
- ✓ Watch those balances from your monthly statements and notice the results as those balances go down
- ✓ Stay focused and realize that this too shall pass – that is, YOUR BAD DEBT RECORD

Here are the instructions to filling out the first schedule:

- ✓ Start off by stating your name and dating the form
- ✓ List your creditors' names, outstanding balances and estimated pay-off dates
- ✓ Before signing the contract, read the <u>large</u> print:
    - Agree to make the payments on time
    - Agree to continue making payments until paid-in-full
    - Agree to not make any major purchases unless absolutely necessary
- ✓ Set a date to treat yourself after meeting a huge reduction in your debt
- ✓ Sign the contract with a witness of whom you trust

Here are the instructions to filling out the second schedule:

- ✓ List your creditors' names
- ✓ Document the original debt amounts
- ✓ Maturity date – sometimes date is set by the creditors
- ✓ Interest rate – see billing statement for information
- ✓ Promise to pay – this date will be set by you; this date should match the date written at "My Personal Payoff Contract." Give yourself a challenge.
- ✓ Document the current ending balance – see your last billing statement
- ✓ Add up the grand totals for the following:
    - The original amount borrowed
    - The promise to pay column
    - The total ending balance – this should <u>match</u> the total on your <u>balance sheet</u> and the total on your <u>net-worth schedule</u>
- ✓ Verify that the promise to pay **monthly amounts** equal the amount noted on your current budget (in the 'debt' expense category)

The term debt has been used loosely but it represents money owed to an individual or to a business. With the current American purchasing life-style which is, *you buy now and pay later*, we are caught up with the theory that it is okay to live beyond our means. With advanced technology, the internet and electronic funds transactions, Americans are able to obtain money more quickly, creatively and they are able to live by their heart's desire.

Here are the New Age ways to regenerating money through debt; note that everything comes with a cost: See a comparative analysis of several loan types at the end of this chapter:

- ✓ Loan Consolidation
- ✓ Tax Refund Loans
- ✓ Payday Loans
- ✓ Car Title Loans

Loan Consolidation is the process of combining all of your loans (debt) into one loan to simplify and possibly lower your monthly payment. By lowering your monthly payment, you are in fact extending your repayment period. Usually, you are instructed that the consolidation is free. And, any fees incurred from the company that will lose your outstanding balance due to the process of consolidation will be paid by the "consolidation" company. To get you hook, the consolidation company will provide you with a calculation of what to expect for the life of your loan. From the new calculated amount of all of your outstanding loan balances, the company will provide you with a *new improved* interest rate and *revised* length of repayment terms. It appears that the consolidation loan may ease the strain on your budget by the lowering of the overall monthly payment. If it sounds too good to be true, then it is. Consequently, the new consolidation loan will lower your interest rate in order to attract you to their business, but you will in essence pay more in interest costs due to the extension of your loan. The end result is that your habits have not changed; you received a quick cure to your past overspending balance, but your problem has not been fixed. In other words, if you take medicine for the "pain" and not figure out what makes you overspend, you will take the extra money relieved from the consolidation and spend it to obtain more debt. If you have this type of debt, you may have a lower payment, but you will stay in debt longer and you will pay the lender more money. This is why the debt consolidation business is thriving. If you have this type of debt, there is hope. You must change your ABCs – attitude, behavior and characteristic. Change your habits, write up a game plan to eliminating debt and stick to it. Go back to the basics and follow the 4-1-1 debt repayment guide.

Tax Refund Loan is the quickest way to access your tax refund money. This fast refund anticipation loan uses your federal income tax refund as collateral and enables taxpayers to access their refund cash almost immediately. Generally, the tax professional and/or lender may require you to file your return electronically (e-filed) with their tax service. While other lenders may require you to provide proof that you have filed and you have received acceptance by the tax authority. After the tax return is prepared and filed, then all interested parties are notified whether or not the tax filer is entitled to a refund. If it is determined that a tax refund is due, then the tax filer is informed of the terms and conditions for receiving the loan. Upon completion of the forms, the loan will be secured and collateralized based on the pending tax refund. The loan applicant (tax filer) will authorize the IRS or some other tax agency to deposit the funds directly into the lender's account. The end result is that the loan applicant will be able to receive within days their tax refund less administrative fees, finance charges, processing fees and interest charges. This loan is difficult to grasp. The tax refund belongs to the person who filed the taxes. Why would you pay extra fees to get your own money? The tax authorities should pay you extra fees for not having access to your money sooner. There are other options to consider in place of a tax refund loan. Here are some options:

- ✓ Pay less taxes during the year – increase your take home pay
- ✓ Eliminate the need for a rapid refund
- ✓ Delay the immediate need by cutting expenses
- ✓ Wait patiently for the refund

If you still have an outstanding debt in this category or you have a habit of obtaining this type of loan yearly then go back to the basics and follow the 4-1-1 debt repayment guide.

Payday Loan is a short-term cash loan based on the borrower guaranteeing a future deposit from their bank account. The borrower would write a personal check for the amount borrowed plus finance charges to receive cash on the spot. The borrower may be asked to sign over electronic access to their bank account. The lenders would hold the check until the next payday. The agreement is to pay the loan and the finance charge in one lump sum. The borrower can redeem their check by paying the loan off with cash. If the loan is not paid in full, the loan will be rolled over until the next pay period. Even though payday loans are extremely expensive, they are easy to obtain. Here are the basic requirements:

- ✓ Bank account in relatively good standing
- ✓ Steady source of income
- ✓ Positive identification

Too good to be true – yes, it is. Loans typically cost 300% annual interest (APR) or more. Payday loans can trap individuals into repeat borrowing due to the extreme high cost, short repayment terms and failing to make good on the check. There are major consequences to not making good on the check used to secure the loan. Failure to repay leads to bounced check fees. Bounced checks can cause bad credit ratings and bad standing at the bank. A bad record can make it difficult to obtain future loans. If you are overcommitted in this category or you feel there is no way out; there is hope. Stop the cycle; accept there is no quick cure. Go back to the basics and follow the 4-1-1 debt repayment guide.

Car Title Loan is secured because it is backed by collateral. The collateral used is your car; this is all you really need in order to get this type of loan. Your credit rating is of no value for this type of loan. In addition, there is really no risk for the lender, since they have access to your title. But, if you were to default on this loan, the lender can do one of two things:

- ✓ Raise your interest rates in order to get even more money
- ✓ Repossess your car and sell it

Title lenders are considered "predatory lenders" because of their unreasonable borrowing terms. A car title loan uses a paid-off automobile as collateral. Usually a car title loan payment is due within a month. You will need to make sure that you can pay off the substantial loan within one to two months. The loan carries a triple-digit annual interest rate and often the amount loaned is far less than the value of the vehicle. At first the interest rate is low, but every month you need the loan to be extended, the interest rate rises to higher levels. This loan can get you fast money, but be aware that if you slip up just a tiny bit, it can result in the loss of your car. If you default on the loan, then the lender will sell it to recoup their money back. If the sale is less than what you owe, you will be on the hook for the difference. If the sale is more than your debt, the lender will keep the profit. Without this debt, the vehicle provides a positive net-worth; yet obtaining this loan causes your net-worth to decrease due to the lost control of your car title and the gain of additional debt. Regain control over your assets while eliminating your debt. Go back to the basics and follow the 4-1-1 debt repayment guide.

New Age Loans Comparison

Various Loan Examples
Using factual information and statistics

To borrow $1,500 and repay at the end of one month:

Type of Loan	Terms	Finance Charges	APR	Total Debt
Emergency Work Loan	2-year work commitment	$ 12.49	9.99%	$1,512.49
Simple Loan	36% APR Cap 3% per month	$ 45	36%	$1,545.00
Credit Card Advance	Interest 23.99% No grace period Upfront 5% fee	$104.86	83.89%	$1,604.86
Car Title Loan	Release title of car No credit check Value of car $5,000 No payment 30-days Paid balance in 35 days Owed extra fees	$365	146%	$1,865.00
Payday Loan	$17.50 fee/$100 15-day term; One rollover	$525	420%	$2,025.00

These calculations were based on the premise that you will pay the full outstanding balance at the end of the month (with one case, balance was paid in 35 days). This sheet was provided to show how quickly debt can become increasingly unmanageable. You cannot change the payment terms of the debt that you have already signed; you can only make smarter decisions moving forward. If you must obtain a loan, do your research first and only sign once you have all of the information and you are extremely comfortable with the payment terms. Do not sign until you have considered all of your options. If you have any one of these loans, other than the employer's loan, make every effort to pay them off first. Do not allow those loan predators to eat up your funds; face them head on and eliminate the debt one-by-one.

CHAPTER E –

Too many expenses – reduce some of them

This chapter is important because the family needs to be aware of their expenses before completing the budget. The family needs to be able to sit down and discuss all of the expenses as well as notate a description of each expense. Each expense needs to have a main label as well as a sub-label. See the categories of the various labels below. Also, the family needs to be aware of the statistics that goes along with a particular expense item. Are you within the spending average of the US citizens with similar income? Are you considering future cost such as inflation? This is not where you input your budget; this is where you **discuss whether an expense item should be added to or deleted from your budget.** The purpose of this activity is to recognize the importance of each expense item needed for every family member before balancing the budget.

Base instructions before introducing the cost for the budget:

1. Select and label your expenses; see explanations of the labels below.
2. Provide a brief description for each of your expense items.
3. Eliminate unused/unneeded expenditures. Start first by eliminating the 'luxury' types and 'nice to have' expense items.
4. Discuss the possibility of reducing the usage in the mixed and variable type expenses.
5. If feasible and possible, pay-down the 'fixed' type expenses.
6. List the final expense items on the budget. (See Appendix: Income & Expense Budget Sheets.)

Expenditure Labels:
N – Item is definitely **"needed".** This item is necessary for survival.
D – Item is considered **"discretionary".** This expense can be reduced.
W –Item is a **"nice to have".** The family members would like to have such niceties.
L – Item is undoubtedly a **"luxury".** The family members would just love to have them.

Expenditure sub-labels:
F – Fixed, the cost does not fluctuate from one period to another. Your rent or mortgage is usually fixed; you pay the same amount from month to month.
V – Variable, the cost fluctuates; usually based on quantity of services provided and items purchased. For example, Mom bought 4 can goods for $1.00. If she had bought 8, the cost would have been $2.00. The cost increases based on the increased in the quantity.
M – Mixed, a mixture of fixed and variable costs. An example would be the "cell phone"; you pay a fixed amount monthly plus a variable rate over the allowed time you signed up for in the contract.

Note: Place the label and sub-label in the box named LABEL below. For example, the expense item, church in my household is labeled N-F as a necessary and fixed item. I pay the same amount weekly to my church and my daughter knows that a portion of her allowance goes to church. This is a required category for my family. Select the right ones for your family below.

Expenses	Category	Label	Brief Description
Church/Holy Temple	**CHARITABLE GIFTS**		
Non-profit Organizations			
Emergency Fund	**SAVINGS**		
Rainy-Day Fund			
College Fund			
Retirement Fund			
First Mortgage	**HOUSING**		
Second Mortgage			
Property Taxes			
Homeowner's (or Renter's) Insurance			
Home Improvement Projects			
Home Furnishings and/or Decorating			
Repairs or Maintenance Fees			

Expenses	Category	Label	Brief Description
Computer/Electronics Service Plans	HOUSING		
Hardware/Software Upgrades			
Storage Fee			
Yard Work/Garden Supplies			
Pest/Termite Control			
Security System			
Association Dues			
Electricity	UTILITIES		
Gas			
Water			
Home Base – Phone			
Cell Phone			
Trash & Waste Mgmt			
Internet Service & Cable			
Grocery list shopping	FOOD		
Convenient shopping			
Appreciation meal out			
Special dining for family			
Fast Food			
Warehouse Clubs Membership			
Vehicle #1 Payment	TRANSPORTATION		
Vehicle #2 Payment			
Vehicle #3 Payment			
Car Insurance			
Auto Club (such as, AAA)			
Repairs and Tires			
Gas and Oil			
License and Taxes			
Vehicle Inspection			
Transit, Tolls and Parking Fees			

Expenses	Category	Label	Brief Description
Child Support	CHILDREN AND PETS		
Tuition/College Expenses			
School Lunches			
School (K-12) Supplies			
Personal Items			
Summer Camp Fees/Supplies			
Sports Equipment and Toys			
Private Lessons, Recitals and Costumes			
Clothing & Shoes			
Dry Cleaning Alterations/Shoe Repair			
Child Care and/or Baby Sitter			
Infant Expenses (such as diapers, etc.)			
Pet Food			
Grooming/Pet Hotel			
Vet Expenses - Shots/Dental/Other			
Pet Training/License/Tags			
Disability Insurance & Long-term Care	MEDICAL/HEALTH		
Health Insurance			
Life Insurance			
Doctor Visits (co-payments)			
Dental Exams			
Vision Exams			
Therapy Expense			
Other Health Exams/Visits			
Medications/Prescriptions			

Expenses	Category	Label	Brief Description
Spousal Support – Alimony	PERSONAL/RECREATION		
Work Clothes/Uniforms/Shoes			
Personal Type Clothing			
Dry Cleaning/Alterations/Shoe Repair			
Toiletries			
Cosmetics			
Hair Care			
Education/Adult			
School Tuition			
School Books and Supplies			
Leisure Courses/Classes			
Subscriptions			
Professional Organization Dues			
Professional Service Fees			
Health Fitness Club Dues			
Sports Equipment			
Gifts, Cards, Flowers			
Entertainment (Movies, Concerts, etc.)			
Vacation			
Unsecured Credit	DEBT		
Secured Loans			
Student Loans			
Extra Credit Line			
IRS Taxes Due			

Here are some statistics regarding the family unit. Data obtained from *US Census Bureau*. These statistics are provided for informational purposes and comparative analysis.

Average age: 48.8 years old (people are living longer)
Number of vehicles owned: 1.9 (round up to 2)
Percent homeowners: 67 percent
Number in family: 2.5 (round up to 3)
Number of earners: 1.3 folks (this indicates that there is usually one bread winner per household.)

Expense Category	Description	Statistics
Charitable Giving	The act of giving anything voluntarily transferred by one to another without compensation; an offering.	People in the income range from $5,000 to $39,999 posted a higher portion of income directed to charitable giving than did any other bracket. Although the people in the $150,000 or more income bracket gave the largest number of dollars to church, religious organizations, and to educational institutions, those dollars represented a smaller portion of income for that bracket that those in the lowest brackets.
Savings	The act of protecting money from loss; setting aside the funds as a deposit to obtain interest income.	Frugal consumers trimmed spending as rising unemployment kept pocketbooks in check and motivated Americans to save. Americans' personal savings rate zoomed to 5.7%, the highest since February 1995.
Housing	The act of covering under shelter; the state of dwelling in a habitation; living accommodations.	Spending on shelter rose over the 1984-2008 period, increasing from 15.9% of total spending to 20.2%.

Expense Category	Description	Statistics
Utilities	The act of receiving public service; such as heat, electricity, water, sewage disposal, etc. The utility usage is based on the age of consumer.	The mean consumption expenditure of households whose head was aged 30 to 59 years old tended to be much higher than the equivalent expenditure of households whose head was either aged under 30 or over 60.
Food	The act of consuming solid or liquid substance used as a source of nourishment to the body.	Food as a proportion of total expenditures decreased from 15.0% in 1984 to 12.8% in 2008. The proportion of household consumption spent on food and non-alcoholic beverages were highest where household incomes were lowest.
Transportation	The act of transporting (moving, transferring) someone from one location to another.	Consumers sharply curtailed vehicle spending due to the recession.
Children & Pets	The act of producing offspring that is considered a son or daughter and a member of the family. The act of obtaining a domesticated animal for companionship and/or amusement; indulged as a member of the family.	Depending on age of the child, the expenses range from $7,580 to $8,570 for families in the lowest income group (income less than $44,500), from $10,600 to $11,660 for families in the middle-income group (income between $44,500 and $74,900), and from $15,490 to $16,970 for families in the highest income group (income more than $74,900).

Expense Category	Description	Statistics
Medical/Health	The act of obtaining physical exams, medical tests, medicine treatments, healing through surgery, preventative health measures and other wellbeing treatments.	Out-of-pocket healthcare spending rose from 4.8% of the total in 1984 to 5.9% in 2008.
Personal/Recreation	The act of purchasing items appertaining to the person for personal comfort and/or desire. The act of recreating, refreshment of the strength and spirits after toil; amusement; diversion; sport; pastime.	Prices for most goods and services generally rise over time but there are some, computers for example, whose prices may actually fall. A spike in gasoline prices may cause consumers to forgo long driving trips, or to purchase more fuel-efficient vehicles.
Debt – how to pay down, (See Appendix: Debt Schedule and My personal payoff contract.)	The act of owing (usually money) and the obligation to pay timely; liability; loan.	Prices for women's apparel rose gradually from 1984 through 1994, and then began to decline, ending the period only about 8% above the beginning level.

Note: The statistics provided above were made available for informational and in some cases an eye opener. This information may be used to assist you in the initial steps of setting up the budget with the guidance of the expense categories listed above.

CHAPTER F –

Financial affairs should be in order!

When I think of the letter "F" – I think about finances. I am consumed by where I am right now. It does not matter whether you are rich or poor, everyone should be working towards something. It's not about how much money you have right now, it's about where you want to be financially. Consequently, you want to get your financial affairs in order if they are not already. If you are not satisfied with where you are right now, then you should be pressing forward full force on the road to becoming financially successful. In this chapter, I will talk about whether your family is moving in the right direction or whether you are stagnant. Also, I will talk about how to get to that financial destination of your dreams. After reading this chapter, you will be able to recognize when you have "arrived"? First, you need to identify your current location. Your balance sheet will make it clear on where you are at any point in time. See a sample balance sheet in the Appendix: Balance Sheet.

Do you have cash or do you have a large amount of unpaid bills? Do you have a savings account or do you owe the IRS? Do you have a working capital for unexpected financial mishaps or will you have to borrow money to cover those unplanned emergencies? The balance sheet tells you at any given point in time where you are financially. It's okay if you are not where you want to be money wise. The key is to recognize where the family is currently "standing", where you need and/or want to be and how long it will take you to get there. Document the over-all plan and the steps it will take to get there. See chapter G to obtain further details on setting goals.

Your financial affairs need to be safely secured in a fireproof safe and a copy needs to be maintained at an off-site location for safe keeping as a contingency plan. Noted below are the documents needed for future valued as well as present valued assets:

✓ ***Proper documentation for future valued assets***
Living trust agreement
Last will and testament
Life Insurance proceeds
Long-term care instructions
Durable power of attorney

✓ ***Proper documentation for present valued assets***
Balance sheet
Net-worth
Working capital
Cash-flow statement
Debt reduction plan
Contracts & note agreements
Income state residual (budget savings)

For each major asset, calculate the related debt to compute the individualized net-worth. Turn to the Appendix: Balance Sheet and the Appendix: Working Capital/Net-Worth sheet to walk through an example and to work through your own personal financial sheet. Here is one example: the net-worth for a house is conservatively valued at $100,000 with a mortgage of $75,000 has a net-worth of $25,000 on your balance sheet. The question regarding where you are financially for this particular asset is $25,000. If you were to sell the house at $100,000, pay off your house debt then you will have a positive cash flow of $25,000. Let's use another example: a car's blue book value may be $15,000 but it has a debt of $18,000; the net-worth is <u>negative</u> at $3,000. To pay the car note off, you may have to dish out an additional amount of $3,000 after selling the car. It may be okay assuming that you have the $3,000 to pay the difference owed. But, you may feel that the car is worth more than $18,000. However, the bottom line is that you owe the creditor more than the car has been quoted by a certified appraisal register system. Therefore, you owe the $18,000 and the car is not considered yours until it is paid in full. Even if you allowed the car to be repossessed for nonpayment of the debt agreement, you will still have to pay off that $18,000. With or without the asset, the debt must be paid. The point to remember here is you want all of your assets' value to be greater than your liability (your debt) to obtain a positive net-worth. With all of this in mind, your assets should be reviewed yearly in order to ensure that your financial movement is upward bound.

For simplicity purposes, the financial affairs represent your piece of the pie. How much of the pie is completely under your ownership? Do you own the pie outright? Are you able to slice the pie, eat it and enjoy it without the creditors irritating you about their "share" owed to them? Let's take one piece of the pie and call it your house. How much of that slice is yours? In other words, what percentage of that slice is "equity"? If you have "equity", leave it alone and let it rise. Don't fall into the trap of obtaining a second mortgage and losing that equity already built up in your house. Instead of half of the pie you could have eaten in "peace", now you may only have ¼ of that slice of pie. What about that car? Do you owe more than it's worth? Well, don't stop making payments on that car. If the car is repossessed, you may still owe money on that car loan even after the car has been sold. The loan company may end up taking 2 slices of the pie, if the value of the car is less than the amount owed. Try to sell the car, if possible, for more than the pay-off loan amount. Another option is to keep the car but speed up your payments; in essence, you are aiming to pay-off the car and to reduce the interest payments at the same time.

Remember, you are not free when a significant amount of the "pie" is due to creditors, particularly when funds are due to old unpaid balances. It is difficult to keep up with the current expenses when most of your incoming funds are due to creditors from purchases made in the past. Here are several examples to help you realize how the cause/effect process works regarding certain financial transactions.

1. A 52' TV bought from Best Buy 10 years ago - you still owe money on it. The television set is not as exciting as it was in the beginning when the unit was first purchased. Yet you are stuck with this unit until it's paid for – eventually.
2. A laptop computer with the latest Windows version - next year a new version will be announced, but you are still paying on the older version. You signed up for the 90-day same as cash program. After 80 days had passed, the family owed more than half of the original amount. The family stopped making payments; interest was applied to the full cost of the computer. To this day, the family still owes money.
3. Complete bedroom suites for a 3-bedroom house - the house will be paid for before the bedroom furniture will be paid-off. The furniture is now valued at less than $2,000.

4. Top-notch exercise unit (used only 4 times last year) - this unit is just collecting dust. Too embarrassed to sell it at a lost.
5. Paying the minimum on past debt - by paying the minimum due, it will take at least 13 years to pay-off the debt. Is this how you want to do it?
6. Bad credit ratings, high interest rates – both are mutually and highly correlated. You pay based on the cash that you have on-hand. The rating is based on how you pay on the outstanding debt and the cash that you are willing to give up to reduce your interest rate. When you have no cash, it is difficult to obtain a lower interest rate that is derived from your current credit rating.
7. Just buying stuff, you don't need. Sometimes, this is okay when you have the excess cash to buy the stuff. When the statement is made regarding excess cash, the assumption is that all bills have been paid and all financial objectives have been met for the current period ending. Never use the credit card when buying stuff you don't need. The main focus is not to incur any interest charges.
8. Too much house for the family's income bracket. Big house with little income will most likely eat up your pie faster than any other expense category. Of course, you should buy a nice house, but you must first consider the members of your household and the total income. You must not forget to review your potential for future income and future needs.
9. Too many cars (or luxury cars) for the number of drivers and the amount of income in the household. Similar to the house, big cars with little income can also eat up your pie. Due to depreciation of this type of asset, the debt chunks do not seem to decrease because the asset value gets smaller and smaller with the passing of time.
10. Not focused on paying off past debt within a reasonable timeframe. Before you bite into the pie, you must review the length of time it is going to take for you to pay off the item(s). Try to conduct this process before you purchase the products and complete this process in the comfort of your own home environment so that you will not become weak and breakdown due to the various store pressures of buying. Consider all of your options, before you even visit the store.

You probably have creditors calling you all times of the day and constantly getting on your nerves. And most, of the mail you get are from creditors threatening you for full payment or statements showing finance charges, late fees and sometimes excessive penalties. There is hope, but it takes a great deal of effort and time. **Here is the key:** stop buying stuff you don't need, pay-off what you owe and only buy what is necessary. Other than a house and car, if you cannot pay off the balance within 90 days (free of any interest fees), then you should question whether you really need the item!!

Get control of that **steering wheel** – this represents your life. Take back your life and **balance** your expenses with your income. This will give you leverage. Release the bondage of not having control of your money. Stop allowing majority of your funds to leave your hands and into the hands of the creditors for those long ago and forgotten pleasures. Free yourself, pay your debt and get back on track by re-focusing on that prize – your dreams.

CHAPTER G –
GOALS are very important

This is the first thing each individual person in the family should complete before anything else is done: set goals. In order to make a change in your life, you must have direction. Allow me to stress the importance to having a purpose in life. Once you realize that you have a purpose, you can now set your path. Well, in order to get where you are going, you need some funds, in other words you need money. Once you have direction in your life, you can no longer spend your money on just anything that is not in the path of your dreams. For example, if your dream is to open and run a restaurant, you cannot spend money on material things that you do not need or items that are non-useful for your purpose. This is considered wasteful and you do not have the time nor the money to waste. Now, you must think as if you are already an owner of this business. You need a building for the restaurant, you need top-notch cooking equipment, you need insurance, and all these items cost money. Your goal now is to obtain sufficient funds to open and operate your dream restaurant. So, why would you spend money on items that are not in the path of your dream, in this case owning a restaurant? Of course, you would not shop for these purchases all at once. You start by taking baby steps, walking slowly and not running, but most importantly you should stay focused. The financially stable individuals are the ones aware of their purpose(s) and they are constantly keeping their eyes on that prize. Now, let's take a moment (close your eyes) and dream. Think about what you want to do in life. Write those dreams down and let's work towards that final "destination". Here is your map – just fill in the gaps!

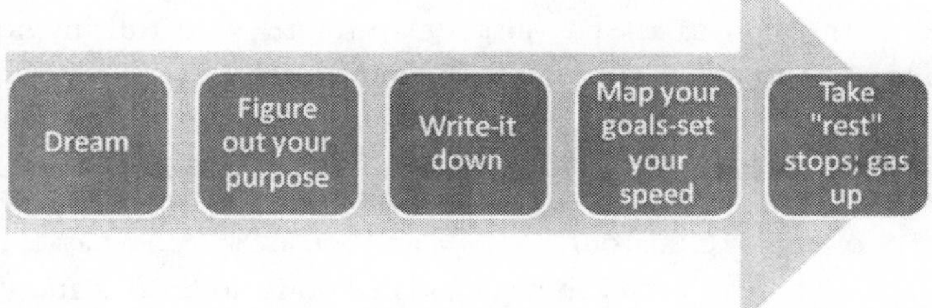

Process 2: Dream to fruition

Just take some time out of your busy schedule and dream. Remember when you were a child; you use to dream about what you were going to do when you became an adult. Now, that you are older, have you accomplished those dreams? If you have accomplished those dreams, then develop some new ones. If you have not accomplished those dreams and you are still interested, then alter the script just a little bit by changing the time-frame and picture a new setting. This is your time; but first you must open your eyes and work out a plan. Do not overwhelm yourself by trying to carry out all of your dreams by the next day. Set realistic goals and take rest stops. It is okay to take breaks every once in awhile.

Foremost, I recommend that you take the time out to figure out your purpose. Pray and meditate to your higher power for your purpose in life. What are the things you need to work through, experience and complete? What marks do you want to leave behind before you check out? Take advantage of this time and ask yourself what are your personal and professional objectives? What goals would you like to implement?

Once you have completed the first two steps, now you must write the objectives down. Document your purpose and make it known to the people close to you. Your trusted party could be your spouse, sister/brother, best friend or a mentor. Note this is the first step in making your dreams seem real, feasible and attainable.

The most difficult step is to map your goals and set your speed limit. This step is where you would document the process flow to meet your goal. You would write down step by step how you plan to reach that goal. The process also includes how long it would take to complete each step. Your steps need to be ordered and adjusted as needed. Remember, there will be events happening along the way to slow you down or even to discourage you from completing your goal. If you get off-track, give yourself permission to a leave (just for a minute) with full intention to return in order to follow through with your dreams.

Let's talk about how to map your goals and to set your speed limit. In order to operate and own a restaurant, you may decide that you need a large cooking oven. The oven may cost around $3,600 and you are able to set aside $1,000 easily each year. This oven can be negotiated down to $3,200 and you are willing to make a deposit of $200 up front. Your goal is to completely pay for this oven within three years. Also, any extra income or bonus money received from this business will go towards the training needed to run a restaurant – this is step two in the process. From this simple example, you now have a glimpse of how to map your dreams. There are three basic steps:

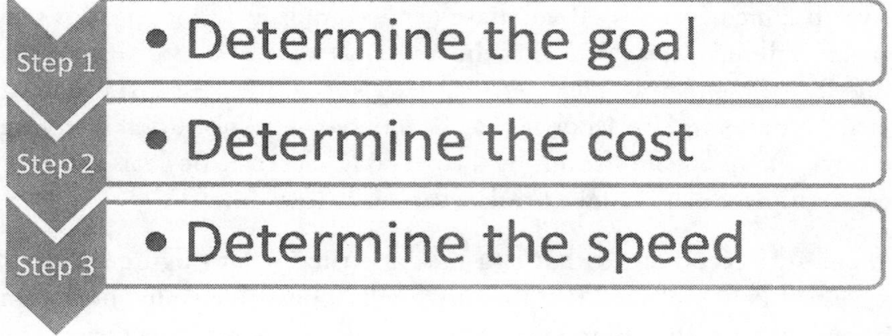

Step 1
• Determine the goal
Step 2
• Determine the cost
Step 3
• Determine the speed

Process 3: Mapping your dreams

These steps are repeated for each major and minor step in the process. You would determine the cost and speed for each high level objective and for each sub-objective for every dream you aspire to implement. If the cost and speed were to go over the documented plan, then make adjustments as needed. Review your goals yearly to make sure that you are still on track.

Lastly, while working towards meeting your goals, you may need to take some "rest" stops and sometimes you may need to just "gas" up. Well, this means that sometimes you are working hard and it appears that you are not moving forward. Sometimes everything that you do to move closer to your final objective puts you back 2-3 steps. You may need a break or a rest stop. There will be other times some folks in your life will only tell you about the negatives of reaching your goal. Some will give you statistics on the chances of this happening to you. Another situation is where the money you were depending on may fall short of your expectations. The process is not happening in the time-frame that you expected. You are frustrated and you want to give up. This is the time to gas up!! Here are some suggestions on how you should gas up:

Process 4: Gas-up time

Take those rest stops and gas up as many times as needed. Just, do not give up. Continue the process until you have completely reached your goal. Once, one goal is completed, go after another, and then another until there is no more to be placed in your tank. Continue to dream, process those dreams, and follow through with those dreams until you have no breath to take or no brain to work through the process. Now, what do you want to do right now? Place the book down for a minute and dream. Don't forget to write everything down. See the Goal Sheet in the Appendix: My Personal Financial Contracts.

CHAPTER HI –

High-valued Inventory (or worthless)

Inventory, inventory, you have so much that the good old Webster Dictionary should have named it "excessive". You probably could tell a "story" about the excessive inventory that you have in your possession. I am sure there is a definite connection to the very first piece of inventory purchased to the last piece purchased probably just yesterday. Here's the question: how much is your stuff worth? Would someone be willing to purchase the item(s) for what it's worth to you or is the value set too high due to sentimental reasons. Well, whatever you have, every family member will need to keep a record of the following for all inventory:

- What you own
- When was the item bought
- A clear picture of the item
- The lifespan of the item
- The original purchase price
- The current value of the item. The current value represents the value that a third party is willing to pay for such a product.

If you own a 8-track player (for example) and it's worth a great deal to you because it was the first thing you bought as a teenager in the 60s, but no-one in the 21st century has heard of it nor has a need for it, then it would be safe to say that your 8-track player is worthless to the third party. You have several options. You may let the item take up space in the attic and collect dust. You may decide to properly discard of the unit and to make room for another item within your budget or you may have a garage sale in hopes that someone like you is crazy enough to purchase what you have. You may even find someone on EBAY, who has an interest for the product. But, it's your call.

Personally, out of all of the areas, this is my weakest area; I have a difficult time letting go of things. Just maybe you are the same way. Nevertheless, I will provide my professional judgment on how to process and record inventory. It will be up to you to monitor it and enforce the high-value inventory in your life. The high-valued inventory (HI) could take over your life, if you allow it. Therefore, you must take control over your stuff. So, be careful not to let the inventory cause you to sacrifice the things that are truly important to you. Okay, let's get started. Make an itemized list of all merchandise, supplies, purchases on hand; hence, an itemized list of goods and valuables with their estimated worth. See Appendix: Home Contents Inventory List. Download extra copies at www.abcsthatmakecents.com.

It is quite okay to maintain inventory that has **no value**, this is assuming that the item is paid for. If you have not fully paid for the item then the item has a {negative} net-worth. Now, the question is whether you want to keep an item that brings the total value of your inventory down. Let's discuss an example. A laptop usually has a lifespan of 3 years or less. If you purchase a laptop and it takes longer than 3 years to pay off the unit then the net-worth would be {negative}. In other words, that asset will equal zero, the liability for that asset will equal to the total amount owed and the net-worth is the difference between the two amounts. Therefore, it behooves you to pay off an item before the life expectancy has met its death bed. Always, beware of the life span of a product that you have possession of or a product that you are considering to buy. This will help you to decide on the payment terms of the product. If the lifespan of your child's bedroom suite is 4 years, then I would recommend that you finance the unit with a 4-year or less payment term. I realize that an 8-year payment term is more appealing because you pay a lower amount from month to month. Nevertheless, I want you to recognize the long-term effect of slowly paying off an item.

I will simplify the example: $6,400 original cost

	- Debt paid off term -		
	1 year	4 years	8 years
Child's bedroom suite (depreciated value)	3,200	3,200	3,200
Outstanding debt	- 0 -	3,200	4,800
Net-worth at the end 2nd year	3,200	-0-	(1,600)

As you can see if you take longer than the life span of the asset to pay-off the debt, then the value will be negative. Make every effort to maintain your assets at zero and above. Also, do not forget to consider interest cost as well as depreciation cost. Of course, it would be difficult to change the payment terms for all of the items in the house at one time. I would suggest that you devise a plan the whole family would be happy with.

Now, take the time out to fill out your inventory worksheet. Make copies of a blank worksheet before hand as you will make changes periodically. Consider the things that you will add to the list. Set a dollar value limit; and, all items greater than that amount will be added to the inventory worksheet. Do not add items that would not be missed if misplaced. For example, I have about 50 calculators. If I were to lose one, I would not fret over it. Start off by adding the big ticketed items, such as a bedroom suite, refrigerator, digital camera, etc. I would not inventory a disposable camera; only add items most important to you so if lost or taken from your personal or home establishment you can consider replacing them. Remember that when you recorded the items at cost, you may be paying more for the value of the items if you decide to replace them at some time later in the future. The items have depreciated and the replacement costs most likely will be higher than the costs you originally paid possibly some time ago.

Set up a process on how you would handle a new purchase. Let's say that first, you would take the product out of the box and put the individual parts together. Once the item is ready to be used, take a picture of that special or unique item and maintain it with the sales receipt and product manual. Store the records in a fireproof safe and/or safe deposit box at a bank. Keep an extra copy of the picture and sales receipt with the inventory worksheet. This may seem like a great deal of work upfront, but after this is completely implemented you will be pleased with the results.

Please make a concerted effort to be conservative when placing a value on each inventory item. This may save you grief in the long run. Also, this is great for insurance purposes as well as for personal reasons. Now, you will finally witness on paper how much your stuff you own and how much this stuff will add to your personal net-worth.

Now that you have all the receipts and/or pictures of the inventory in your house and in other storage locations, you are now ready to total up the inventory on the worksheet. Try to conduct this activity around Fall or Spring break so that the whole family can participate and feel involved in the process. Make the activity fun by taking snack breaks and laughing at the things you have found that you forgot you had. Complete the inventory by location and consolidate the various inventory lists to one final worksheet.

Now, it is time for the coding of the inventory. Set up a system on how the family will agree on the following inventory codes. See the categories below:

X	Item will be disposed of… set a date, such as Summer 2012
Y	Item will be fully evaluated at the next inventory review time
Z	Item will be maintained as it is needed
XY	Item will be contributed to a much needed organization by 12/31
XZ	Item will be sold through… (State the source)
XYZ	Item will be upgraded or replaced as it is in the budget

If your plan is to get rid of something, then code it "X". If your plan is to keep the item, then code it "Z". Most items will probably be code "Z", as these items have a purpose and are much needed by the family unit.

In addition to coding the inventory by the various combinations of X, Y and Z, also mark each item with a GREEN or YELLOW highlighter and/or a RED pen. Use a RED pen to mark the X items, YELLOW to highlight the Y items and GREEN to highlight the Z items. Do not be afraid to do this; conduct this procedure as quickly as possible. Get rid of those RED items promptly, before you do anything else. Trust that once you have completed this, you will be happy because those items were not even as gratifying as you thought. You will not miss them – they were outdated anyway.

Last step is actually striking out (with the RED pen) the inventory items disposed, contributed, sold and replaced as directed by you and noted in the inventory worksheet. Great, you have done a superior job; pat yourself on the back.

CHAPTER JKL –

J-Just K-Keep L-Levelheaded!!

This is where you learn how to keep level headed with little to no money. Here is the key. You must set spending limits which means that you must set up a budget. Out of all of the chapters in this book, you absolutely must comprehend and follow this chapter. Let's say that you are driving on the expressway, and you come up on a speed limit sign stating how fast you are allowed to go. Now, if you are 5 miles or less over the speed limit, you may get a warning, 6-15 miles over the limit, you may get a $75.00 ticket and greater than 15 miles over the limit, you may go to jail. Well, this is similar to spending money. When you are given your payroll check, you must recognize upfront where the funds will be allotted to and how much before you cash that check for any particular pay period. As I am confident that most of you are aware, you personally do not have any leg room to go over your regular paycheck and the banks will not cover you even if you were to go over by just ONE penny. If you have a savings account, the bank may pull funds from that account assuming that you have sufficient funds. Under the new law, with your approval, the banks can accept checks even if you do not have the funds, but they will charge you an "insufficient funds" fee. Now you are stuck with paying the bank fee in addition to the original check amount. If you do not approve of this process, then the check will be returned to the sender for you to come face-to-face with the person and/or company with great embarrassment, because you were not even able to cover the check amount. Not having adequate funds could cause your check(s) that you have written to "bounce". In other words the checks will not clear the bank. When one check bounces it seems as though all of the others will following suit, leaving the account in a state of continuous "bouncing" mode. This is considered the bouncing check syndrome. And, it is very difficult to get back on track. Fortunately, we live in a land of opportunities and second chances. But, before you write another check, <u>set up a budget, manage your income and watch your expenditures so that you can reverse the behavior of writing bad checks.</u> Decide upfront who you are going to pay first and never second guess yourself once that decision is made. Carry the budget wherever you go.

Make sure that you read chapter E-expenses to ensure that you consider all of the various expense categories. Also, the back of this book provides a blank worksheet at Appendix: Income & Expense Budget Sheets.

Before getting started, make sure that you understand the following key terms:

- Routine (required) payments – These are the necessary expenses for basic survival. For example: mortgage expense, apartment rental, required insurance costs, utilities, etc.
- Necessary with some discretion – Examples would be: food, clothing and transportation. Of course, you would need transportation to get to work, but do you really need a high priced vehicle that requires premium gasoline. Also, do you need "steak" to survive or is "hamburger" sufficient?
- Discretionary expenses – Personal and recreational expenses of which can be considered a luxury. This is the first category to look at when it is necessary to cut expenses.
- The future or the thinking of others category – Examples would be: savings, retirement plans, and contributions/giving. This is the category that I would recommend you set funds aside first before you spend in the other categories.

The bottom line is to advise that you are given a whole "pie" and it is up to you to decide how you will slice it up. If you spend it all in one category, such as having a fancy car with high insurance cost, you may not have enough to purchase suitable clothes to maintain a decent job. Remember, it is your pie; once eaten, it's gone.

How do you stay "level headed"? Well, first you list your various expenses by categories:

Level 1 -Basic expenses for your survival
(i.e. personal type and place to lay your head)

Level 2 -Required but in moderation
(i.e. food for the nourishment of your body, not junk food or alcohol)

Level 3 -Necessary for the convenience of life
(i.e. automobile for faster access to work, church, school and home.)

Level 4 -Wanted expenses
(i.e. cable TV)

Level 5 -Luxury expenses
(i.e. obtaining top of the line or having more than what's needed/wanted)

Here are the steps to setting up the budget and staying level headed:

Step 1: Pay yourself (and each family member) an allowance.
Step 2: Add up all income from guarantee sources.
Step 3: Set up budget - allocate the funds starting with level one (see above).
Step 4: Discuss with family members what it takes to be level-headed.
Step 5: If there are any left-over funds – agree on what to do with the leftovers.

Provided below is a pie of the average percentages spent by category that depicts how most families stay level headed: A blank pie is provided as an extra visual aid for you to complete located at Appendix: A Piece of the Pie. Slice the pie that best fits your family.

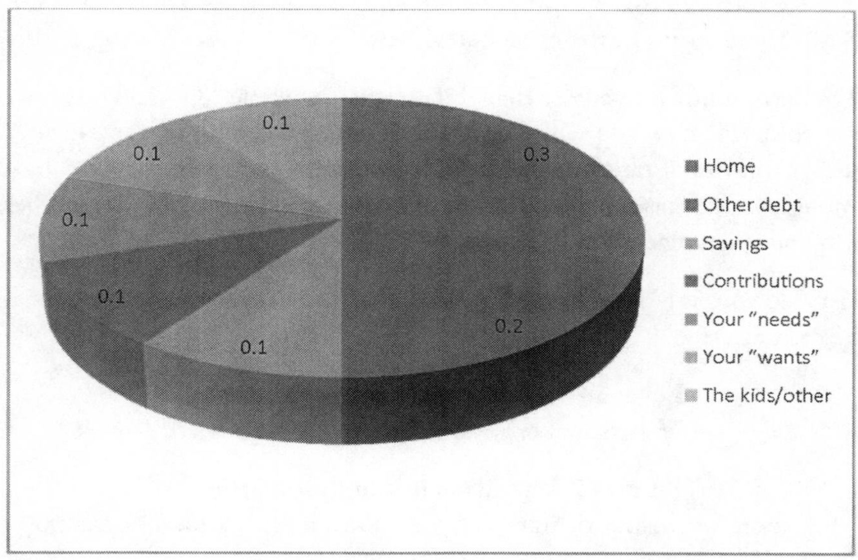

Process 5: Standard Pie Percentages

There are tons of expenses to spend your money on, but you have only one pie for each pay period. If you place most of your funds in the house, then you will have less to spend on other needs and wants. If you have no debt, then you have more money to spend on the other categories. Therefore, choose your expenses and manage your categories wisely. When given funds during a pay period, stay level headed and do not consume more than is allotted. Take the time out to slice the pie slowly and carefully. Consider the levels of spending and follow the steps of budgeting. Once the pie is sliced, the contract signed or legal agreement made, you cannot go back and unsliced the pie. If you have extra slices left-over, try reflecting on freezing the remains in a savings account to be used on future needs and goals. Setup an expectation of when the remaining slice(s) will be used. Do not and I repeat, do not bite into the slice before obtaining the available funds in your hand. Remember, once the pie is eaten, you must wait until the next pay period before you get another one. Do not stress out if your pie is not big enough, there may be more to be dished out during the next pay period. If you still cannot work with the size of your pie, then you must find ways to either increase your income or decrease your expenses. The good thing to note here is that you have options, just stay level-headed.

Once the budget is set, this is not the time to go out and spend all your money in one sitting. You must follow this process before making a purchase:

A. Set up the budget.
B. Agree on a timeframe for each purchase as needed.
C. Pick at least 3 quotes and compare the choices selected.
D. Review the choices before making the final decision.
E. Negotiate the best purchase price with added options.
F. Make sure you read the fine print.
G. Purchase the item but stay within the budget.
H. Enjoy your purchase and regularly review its "worth".

Later on in the book you will learn the importance of carrying your spending license along with your budget everywhere you go. The best part is that you will have the opportunity to fill in your spending license. This is a joint family adventure. Now is not the time to skip steps. Follow the chapters, one step at a time and stay level-headed.

CHAPTER MN –
Monitor your Net-worth

This chapter is noted as the eye opener chapter. This is where you find out how much you are worth. What is net-worth? Net-worth is the total of all of your assets minus the total of all of your liabilities (debt). In other words, **net-worth is the difference between the value of what you own less the value of what you owe.** So, what do you own and how much do you own? Follow along by referencing the balance sheet & the net-worth worksheet noted at Appendix: Balance Sheet and Appendix: Working Capital/Net-Worth sheet.

There are folks that feel they are "worth" a great deal because of the certifications, degrees attached to their name or the number of people they know in the community. I do not disagree with this, but given all things financial, and for purposes taken from the financial world, I will be discussing only the tangible aspects of net-worth. When I say net-worth, I mean having ownership of the physical assets outright? In other words, net-worth is derived from assets less the amount of debt still owed. Sometimes, net-worth is derived from debt where the assets are no longer owned. Net-worth can be positive as well as negative. Also, you can have a net-worth of zero. Monitoring your net-worth is necessary to ensure growth is happening by **at least one dollar yearly**. And, I suggest that you do not maintain a net-worth that is zero or less.

When you buy an asset, it is imperative that you review the long-term value of that asset. If, for example, you purchase an item that will not have a long-term value, then you ought to make sure that you completely pay for the item before the value of the asset reaches zero. Listed below are several examples for your consideration. Take heed and make an effort to change your ways if these examples fit you. These are absolute No-no's:

a. Going to a restaurant (in particular, a fast-food restaurant) to buy a quick meal, using a credit card and not paying the item off when the bill comes.

b. Purchasing gas with a credit card with the intention not to pay off the balance when the statement arrives.
c. Paying for a movie (or some other entertainment) with a credit card and not setting aside the money to pay the bill in full to eliminate the interest charges.
d. Buying much needed merchandise with a credit card and taking longer than the life of the products to pay off the bill. For example if you buy lotion with a credit card, it should not take longer than three months (at most) to pay off the product. Usually, when you buy a 16-oz bottle of lotion, it probably will last approximately 3 months. Here's the situation: when you add that $7.99 plus tax, cost of the lotion, to a credit card which already has a large balance and you are unable to pay it down by the end of the pay cycle, then you are, in essence, paying interest cost on that lotion. Since the balance is too high to pay it off by the end of the month or payment cycle, and you are unable to pay the full balance, you now have added the cost of the lotion to the list to be calculated for interest costs. Therefore, next month not only will you owe that balance from the previous statement, but also, you will owe that $7.99 + tax + other activity + interest on the total unpaid amount. In three months, you would have used up the lotion, yet the balance remains unpaid in addition to paying interest cost. Was the lotion worth the extra cost? The excess paid over and above the cost of the item is considered negative. This is a negative amount and it reduces your net-worth as it reduces your available cash. In addition, it increases your debt. This is a double whammy which can also jeopardize your positive net-worth.

Also, note that the value of knowing your net-worth is not so that you can brag to "The Joneses." This net-worth figure is your bargaining tool to obtain other things at the discounted rate, at your leisure and pleasure. I am sure you are aware that when you have a little something on the side of positive net-worth, you can effortlessly add other assets that will increase your net-worth. In other words, when you own something that adds to your portfolio, you can easily add more things. Let me to break it down some more, a high net-worth allows you to buy more assets with no down-payment through your increased 'credit rating.' This chapter will show you how to use your allotted funds wisely in order to acquire those desirable things on your wish-list. Of course, this assumes all expenses are within the budget. In essence, **you need to maintain a <u>positive</u> attitude, preserve your <u>positive</u> goods, diminish those <u>negative</u> transactions, and sustain a <u>positive</u> net-worth** by upholding the following rules for those new purchases:

A. Set up a budget to be used regularly.
B. Agree on a timeframe to purchase the items in the budget.
C. Pick at least 3 quotes and compare the choices selected. **Investigate for the best deal.**
D. **Review** the choices before making the final decision. Do your research.
E. Negotiate the best purchase price with added options **(such as a 90-day payment, same as cash agreement).**
F. Make sure you read the fine print. If necessary, go back to the drawing board to **ensure nothing is missed.**
G. Purchase the item while staying within the budget.
H. Enjoy your purchase and regularly review its "worth."

To improve upon your net-worth, you must match up the life of the assets with the term of the debt. Items that have a life of one week or less should be paid with cash or a debit card. If you use a credit card, you must pay the balance off in full to eliminate any interest costs. Listed below are examples of expense categories with a very short-term (one week or less) life span:

- Eating out
- Purchasing gasoline
- Grocery shopping
- Local entertainment (such as movies, concert, etc.)

Items that have a <u>life span of one month or less</u> may be paid with a credit card assuming that the balance will be paid in full when due. Note the payment terms are set by your creditors. You may be better off by paying for the following items with <u>cash</u> and not credit:

- Merchandise such as lotion, deodorant, household cleaning items, etc.
- Minor maintenance work such as auto oil change, replacing small parts, etc.
- Insignificant home upkeep work such as replacing the air filter, light bulb, etc.

- Utility, Internet and cable bills
- Prescription and over-the-counter medicine

Sometimes situation warrants you to leave a balance on your credit card statement, such as unemployment, sickness to the bread-winner, or even death. In these situations, try to **analyze the cost of using your credit versus the cost of using your savings.** Analysis would include, but not limited to, the increase of interest expense for charging the items versus the decrease of interest income for using the savings account.

Now, some items have a <u>shelf life of approximately a year</u>. These items may use a longer payoff program to pay off the items. If you cannot take advantage of the 90-day same as cash then set up a plan on how you will pay off the balance. Here are some examples of items that have a longer term shelf life. I still recommend paying off the balance as soon as feasibly possible.

- Major auto repair work
- Travel with hotel and air-fare
- Medical services such as an operation
- Major home improvement work
- Insurance cost

Classify the assets that have a much longer shelf life to match the expected liquidity of that asset. For instance, if you expect the life of an asset to be 3 ½ years, then you should plan to pay off the debt for that item in less than 3 ½ years. I am not suggesting that you take your time paying off a debt because it has a long shelf life. I am saying that if you cannot pay all of your debt off in one month, then pay down your debt within the shelf life of the asset. Here are just a few examples:

- A personal computer with a life of 3 years
- A vehicle with a life of 6 years

Your house most likely is your highest-valued asset. Chances are that you will live in one house for most of your adult working years. Therefore, it makes since to have a longer paying agreement with the mortgage company. With this in mind, if you plan to live in your house for X number of years and you plan to have income to sustain the mortgage payments, then it appears reasonable to have a mortgage with X years to maturity. I am not advocating taking your time to paying off your home mortgage as it seems that you will stay there for the majority of your life. I am suggesting that you set up a mortgage with the intention to pay off sooner to reduce the interest costs. Start off by paying twice a month or paying more than the amount is due and adding the excess to the principal balance. **Take small steps to make your net-worth increase yearly.** Constantly, review your assets and liabilities (debt) to ensure that you are getting your money's worth. After reviewing and summarizing all of your assets and liabilities, you will know your net-worth. Are you content with where you are now? If not, set-up a plan to work towards growth while enjoying the quality of life's treasures.

CHAPTER O –
Standard Money Operation

Operation – cash flow – flow chart: See Appendix: Statement of Cash Flows & Appendix: Cash Calendar.

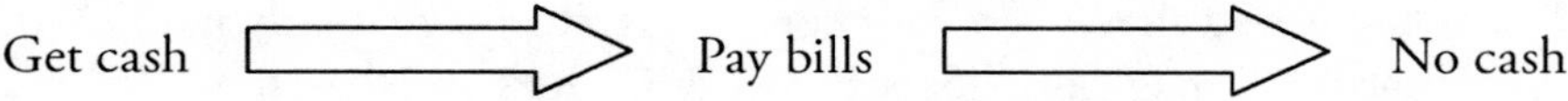

You are probably acquiring more knowledge each and every day in regards to your standard of operation on how you process those financial transactions in good and bad times. You operate a certain way when you obtain money. Sometimes when you get a check, it's already spent; all you need to do is sign it and hand it over. Sometimes you take the check straight to the bank and deposit it in order to pay the bills for that period. There are some folks who would take the check and deposit some of the funds in their savings account and the remainder amount is deposited into the checking account. What is your standard operation? Generally, an individual's standard operation is pretty much set by the time they reach high school (9-12 grades) and permanently set by the time they reach adult-hood (18-20 years old). It is based on the people that are a part of your home environment and folks within your close niche surroundings. How your mother, father, and/or grandparents handle the flow of money will determine how your children will handle money. Some folks' standard operation for incoming and outgoing cash is handled swiftly, while others process their funds slowly. Well, it doesn't matter if you have a massive amount, small amount or no amount, your standard operation will be the same based on your internal upbringing and teachings. For example, if your standard operation is to always keep your creditors informed on how and when you expect to pay your bills, then when you do not have the funds, you will continue to contact your creditors on your current situation. I am not a physician, but I will tell you that your upbringing is connected to how you spend your funds. In addition to your mind, which is nourished through your family and friends, your body will have a huge effect on your "money operation." Those vasoconstrictors, which cause the opening of your blood vessels to narrow, also can have an effect on your money operation. Those chemical substances, your nerves, adrenaline, body temperature, angiotensin, body tension and quite often stress will have a great effect on your M-O-N-E-Y operation. You may not feel the warm flow of your blood, but that flow affects the body organs and the body recognizes when the blood is not flowing smoothly. Therefore, the level of smoothness of your internal system will have a significant effect on the money flow and how you "operate" with and without money. So, it should be clear that there is a direct and positive correlation between the "wellness" of your mind, body and soul and the "deepness" of your funds. Please be assured that when your complete system is regularly nourished, your funds will magically flourish greatly in the same direction. With a healthy makeup, you will be better able to operate and work on/through the amount of money that's available to you. Once your body is operating properly, then will you have a clear head to be able to work through those tough situations.

Now, it is very important to take the time out of your busy schedule to understand your unique standard of operation. In addition, each family member must understand their own standard and the head of the family must identify how the family can come together as one unit with the various operational styles. Here are some techniques on how to start studying yourself as well as your family. I suggest that you make every effort to figure out how the family operates when they get their hands on some money:

- ❖ Do you spend more when you are hungry?
- ❖ How do you spend when you are happy or sad?
- ❖ Do you manage well when you are upset?
- ❖ Is your stress level high when you have less than the required amount to pay the bills?
- ❖ What is your course of action when you do not have the funds to pay the bills by the due date?
- ❖ What do you do when you get extra funds? How do you spend a bonus check or a tax refund check?
- ❖ Generally, are you considered a big spender or a big saver?

If you were raised to depend on others to get you through the tough times, then you will go to the folks you trust to pull you out of that hole even when it is not "knee deep." If you were raised to search out for available resources, then you will follow those agencies' policies and procedures so that you are able to obtain those needed funds. If you were raised to solely depend on yourself, then you will go after any means necessary to get over and out of that hole. If you were taught to do without when you lack funds, then you will do just that. And, vice versa, when you obtain extra funds, you will watch and follow suit based on how others close to you spend their money. Your attitude is the same with and without funds. You follow what you know and your actions are based on what you have learned as a youngster.

If you are anything like me, it takes a great deal of effort to make a change. Sometimes it is difficult to unlearn what you have been doing most of your life. Therefore, I recommend maneuvering around your makeup versus trying to totally eliminate your unique way(s). For example, if you tend to spend more money when you are upset then do not go to the store at that time. Send someone else in place of you going. Case-in-point, I am aware that I will get a bonus check on April 15th and I have been informed on how much I will get for all the hard work of me completing income tax returns for the year. As soon as I get home, I will sit down and review my budget and long-term term goals to see what I really need at this point in time. I do not watch any TV commercials or read any sales paper advertisements to deter me from writing down my own personal goals and budget. Once, I make a decision on what to do with the extra funds, I will adjust my budget to show that future increase. I will not make any commitments nor spend the money before obtaining the funds; I will wait patiently for the check to arrive. **My future plans will be completely documented before the check arrives in my mailbox.** If I get a check unexpectedly, I will deposit it into the bank. I will not spend the money; I will not pass go until I have reviewed my personal goals and long-term plans. Now, it is your time to follow this example; read further to know what tools are needed.

Let's talk in more detail about this so-called "money" operation. What worked well in the 1920s may be lacking in 2010. Also, what worked well while in school with no children may not be sufficient when you have several children under your roof. Now, some things may never change like the size of the dollar bill or even the face on the bill, but what you can buy with that 'one' dollar bill may change. So, let's talk about the flow of money. <u>You get money in; you pay bills, save some, and spend the rest.</u> In short, this is the proper standard to have assuming that you are able to access enough money to cover the remaining steps. What if you have a deficit amount of funds to continue to the end of the money operation line? How should one operate without enough debt-free funds to flow to the end of the money operation process? Should you borrow the money or take what you need by any means possible? Should you contact the creditors or ignore them completely? Should you have trust in a higher power or should you just give up? Continue reading, there is hope.

I will show you in simple terms how to "operate" on your money. Remember, this is a slow process. Note it takes time to bake a cake from scratch. Similarly, it will take time to operate on your money. Planning is the key. Actually it takes four (4) Ps to complete the money operation. Read 'The P Chapter' to learn about how the process may be slow. Right now, let's continue with the main OPERATION.

You need the following tools before you operate:

1. The calculator, paper and pencil
2. The plan (short term and long term)
3. The budget
4. The revised plan and budget
5. The spending license
6. The permission slip

Before you move forward, you will need to "wash" your hands and make sure your whole household's hands are clean. Clean them from the "dirt" performed in the past. Sanitize them by correcting the errors made and notifying the appropriate parties for retribution. Note that it takes time to <u>wash away</u> the filth from past operations. <u>This is a symbolic notification</u> to your mind/body that you are moving forward in the proper matter. In essence, you will operate with the funds given to you earnestly and you will deduce funds due to others accurately and swiftly. Once you have cleaned and dried your hands, now it's time to grab hold of that calculator and get to work.

<u>Step One: The calculator, paper and pencil</u>

Obtain that calculator, paper and sharpen your pencils. The operation must take place with all individuals in the household; it is necessary that each member be provided a job in order to feel a part of the family's "money" operation. Before you sit down to operate you will need to decide how much income you take in on a routine basics, list your expenses and the family's individual goals. This will help you to complete the budget. Check your vital signs, every 5-15 minutes to ensure a successful operation. The overall vital signs are based on subtracting the total expenses from total income. If you have more expenses than income, STOP and check your vitals and PUMP out some of those expenses. Make sure everyone in the family is breathing, because it may be very difficult to CUT out some of the expenses without the family members' help. Some of the expenses are personal and it may not be easy to detach from them. Yet, this step is crucial and necessary to be able to move to step #2 – planning for the future.

Step Two: The plan (short term & long term)

Develop a rough draft of your dreams, goals, aspirations and purpose in life. This may be rough to put together because you have not put together your budget. You do not know if you are even able to meet your basic expenses. Have you ever watched those TV shows regarding doctors and nurses at the hospital? Sometimes the program shows a scene on what the doctors and nurses do in preparation of the risky but crucial operation. They role play on how the operation should be performed before the big event. They discussed the steps in the operation, where they will cut and what the level at which the vital signs should be checked. This is similar to your initial step of setting your plan. Think about and meditate on those dreams that you look forward to accomplishing. Separate the long-term goals from the short-term ones. Long-term goals are dreams that you want to accomplish, but may take longer than a year. Write down all of your goals with the foresight that these goals may change. Some will be added onto the main list and others will be crossed out. Just write down your initial thoughts with estimated costs and timeframe to completing those dreams.

Step Three: The budget

Focus on setting the budget for the current year. Add up the income and deduct your expenses. See a blank budget sheet located at Appendix: Income & Expense Budget Sheets in the back of the book. If your expenses are higher than your total income, try to flush out some of your expenses. If you feel that you cannot eliminate or reduce some of your expenses, consider looking at ways to increase your income. The key thing to recognize is that sometimes when you increase your income, there may be a direct correlation with some other expense category. Some expenses will automatically increase when income is increased. For example, when you take on a second job, you may need to hire a baby-sitter to keep the children or pay extra for a day-care. Before you say yes to a second job, you should consider the net financial effect due to the extra income. If you get that extra job making $150 a week and the after-school care will cost $70 a week, you will need to ask the following question: Is it worth getting the second job when your net income for that job will be $80/week? This will be a question that your family will answer together.

Once you have cut out and eliminated those desirable, yet not needed expenses and you have a positive flow internally and externally, then you will be ready for the next step of the operation. Now, breath – the budget is the hardest part of the operation. You are due for a celebration – please do not blow your budget, at this point in the process. Maybe have a toast by using white cranberry juice as your drink. Try not to drink too much of the juice; you may want to use it at the end of the operation.

Step Four: The revised plan and budget

Fine tune the plan and budget. There will be a need for some residuals for this phase of the operation. The remaining funds that are left over from the previous step should not be thrown away. You should not spend the remaining funds on senseless items such as buying things that are not in the budget, unplanned for or not approved in advance by the family members. Yes, the operation takes more than one family member to succeed and complete. All parties must contribute to the efforts and each party is responsible to the others for the efforts given to them. If you are a one man/ woman shop then I suggest you set strict goals for yourself since no one is governing your spending unless you have a trusted friend to guide you through the steps of the "operation." Nevertheless, the individual unit will still need to follow the steps of the operation as set forth in this chapter.

This is the step used to seal the deal. This is where you finalize your goals, dreams and/or aspirations. Make the decision on whether you wish for something small or something huge. Would you like to obtain that second degree or a vacation home? Have you always wanted a boat to sail around the world or would you just like to go on a cruise. This is the time to just take a moment and dream…close your eyes and speak out your desires. Do not interrupt the others while they are speaking, just relax – your time is coming. This is what the "residual" amount is for. The leftovers, the excess funds will be used for long-term goals. Again, long-term goals are dreams that you want to accomplish, but may take longer than a year. The length it will take to implement a goal will depend on the amount of your residual, the total funds needed, the commitment level and fortitude.

What is your "staying power" to make it to the end of the operation? Remember, you must not leave the operating table until everything has been sealed. Also, note that after the operation has been sealed, you will still need to add a stitch or two for increases/decreases of funds that may occur during the year.

Long-term goals are today's dreams that will come to pass in the far future. The funds are set aside routinely (by you) in order to meet the annual expectations of the goal(s). For example, if you plan to buy a house in five years and you would like to have a $10,000 down payment, then you will need to set aside at least $2,000 annually to reach that goal. The goals set must be realistic and feasible. But, you must want it so bad that you are <u>willing to put in your whole mind, body and spirit to make that dream come true</u>? Are you willing to wait five years or more to meet your heart's desire? What if there is a bump in your life and you have to place your dream on 'hold'. It appears that you will miss a couple of those payments to meet that annual expectation. You should not give up but continue on the pure hope that you will get there eventually. Continue where you left off, establish again that "staying power" until the operation is complete.

If you are uneasy with setting a long-term goal, then set some short-term goals. For example, you may want to purchase a $500 dollar video camera by the end of the year. Your plan is to set aside $50 each month until you have enough to purchase that camera. Open up an account and set aside funds for those short term goals as well. Don't forget to check your vital signs. Make sure your adrenaline is flowing. Pat yourself on the back; you have completed steps one through four of your new way of operating. Well, now that you have documented and signed those short and long term goal sheets, the next objective is to seal the deal and check for changes annually. <u>My recommendation is for you to review your objectives when you go for your annual physical or annual checkup.</u> Remember that your body health affects your financial health. While you are waiting in the doctor's office, look over your personal goals to ensure that you are on track.

<u>Step Five: The spending license</u>

To move forward, you must maintain a spending license. You have completed your budget, you have completed your personal goal statement, you are almost ready to close up and finalize the operation. This step and the final step are unique tools that were established in order to have some type of mini-spending identification with you at all times. This spending license or picture ID is to be used as a paper document for minor and major expenditures in an effort to slow the family's spending down in this fast pace world. No one in the family can spend money without such an ID card. The license is used to identify you, show your cash allowance and illustrate for the family their spending class level. The various spending classes are given in Chapter Q. In Chapter Q, it is suggested that you complete a quiz by following the steps; nevertheless, there is no passing or failing score, there are only levels in which you can spend your money. The license will show you what your spending allowance should be for each period as well as whom to contact in case you become weak and you want to spend more than what's allotted in the budget. You must follow the instructions specifically as you do not want to leave the stores with items not in your budget. Use Chapter Q to assist you in a step-by-step process to the workings of the budget. Just remember that it is crucial for you to complete the budget before you are able to take your picture ID. Afterwards, review and complete the Appendix: Spending ID Card & Instructions at the back of the book.

Step Six: The permission slip

A permission slip will be required in order for each family member to spend money at any given store. This is the time to receive the necessary approvals from the head and co-head before spending. The designated family heads will need to approve the expenditures noted on the permission slip before going to the store to make those major and minor purchases. The permission slip will provide the member's authorization to spend at a particular store for a particular item(s). This is agreed upon in advance, before you leave the house. Please note that you cannot leave home without your "spending license" and "permission slips." The family may also set limits on spending amounts without a permission slip, but **you must always carry your license**. See Appendix: Minor Purchase Pass and Appendix: Permission Slip to Spend.

Well, it looks as though you have completed the money operation and you have some cash leftover. You may now pass go and celebrate; but, do not forget that you cannot spend more than what's in the budget. A summary of the whole process has been provided for your convenience.

<u>The summary statement and flow chart</u>

Operation – cash flow – flow chart

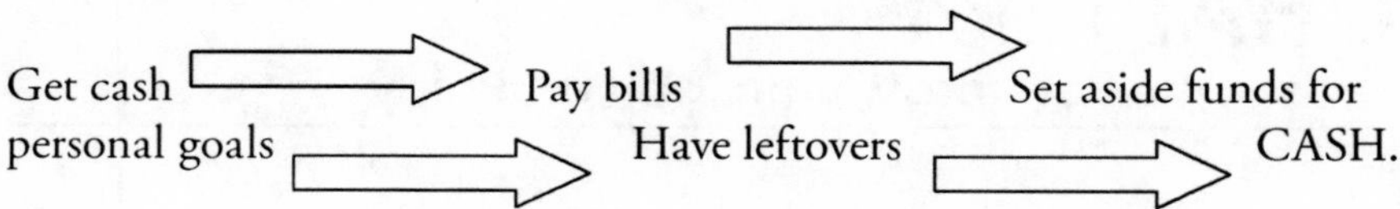

Process 6: Cash Flow Operation

Seal the process by closing up. Return to the beginning when there is a change to any of the functions noted above. Continue to check your vitals in order to ensure there is always cash on hand. Well done, you have completed a successful financial operation. Now you are able to get ready for the next operation. The term 'operation' represents the accomplishment of a goal. **<u>A successful operation is when you are paying your bills, achieving your goals and still have some leftover cash to spare.</u>** Once one operation is complete, set new goals and prepare the family for the next operation. It is similar to a roller coast, you go up with cash, then you go down (slightly) by paying your bills with strong consideration to your goals and with the leftovers you start the process all over again. Work your personal roller coaster by using the Cash Calendar provided in the Appendix.

CHAPTER P –

Peas in the Pot - pray, plan, pay and play

Through previous presentations, class participants are shown *live demonstrations* on how to take the "P" from Penny and use my invention called the 4P-system. Being seasoned in the financial world and with my personalized ups and downs, I have developed my own system. The focus of my 4P system is to place value on 4 key words that begin with the letter P. First you pray, then you plan (budget), then you pay (bills) and finally you play. I guess, I forgot one major P – you need to get PAID. Basically, everyone should value and price these major Ps to fit their family lifestyle. In my personal example, I was walking out to my unpaid new car with my walking papers; my thoughts were that I was sure going to miss getting PAID. Would I still PRAY? Not to mention planning for the future – especially paying those bills – and would I be too depressed to play. We all must "play" sometimes, but on the 8th day of May, my path was being redirected again and being laid off was not a playing matter. It appears that I was starting over again, my new beginning, my personal struggle. I needed to personally learn how to endure with the high prices in the current environment as an educated, unemployed single parent. God wanted me to fully understand what others have gone through and what others are currently going through financially. With this new knowledge base, I am better able to educate others on how to PRESS forward and keep the FAITH even though you cannot see what's ahead. I am learning how to allow God to direct my path. Please allow me to teach you how to balance the budget and to enjoy yourself, even when you feel you are lacking or missing some of the Ps. Above all, continue to pray by asking the Lord to show you how to manage even when there is metaphorically speaking only one P left in the family's money pot.

How do you pay the bills and enjoy what you have? How do you spread out the Ps so that the funds can last until you get PAID again in order to enjoy what's remaining in the batch? First, I need to show you how to balance the budget. <u>Balancing the budget is as simple as counting the pennies that you have</u> and dividing them up based on the number of days in a pay period and the number of family members in the household. Nevertheless, you must remember that you cannot give out more than the income that you have to give. In other words, do not spend more than the income you bring home. It does not matter who's asking; you cannot release (or promise to pay) something that you do not have.

Okay, now bend down and attempt to start the juggling of the pennies. This is the time to gather up the family to discuss how you plan to divide up the funds. Make sure you have plenty of paper to take notes because each expense item needs to be discussed separately and collectively. A pencil is needed for each family member. Also, this is the time to PRAY and PLAN for your future. Use as many biblical scriptures as necessary; the bible will be your reference guide.

Here is a list of questions to ask the family when discussing the expenses:

1. Does the family really need this expense item for this year?
2. How much of the expense item is needed for this time period?

Do not give up even after some time has passed during the family discussion. Continue with patience while prioritizing your expenses. Review your available credit (or capital) and consider your options. This can give you some hope. Be mindful to add some "play time"; this may include taking a small break. It's okay if the "play" time is mixed with the business of setting up the budget. Just recognize that the budget represents the income less the expenses. Do not allow yourself to fall in the trap of 'I got to have it now.' Objectively consider whether or not the expense is an absolutely needed expenditure. But at the same time, you should include some budgeted item(s) for personal relaxation. Balance your Ps: PRAY, PLAN, PAY, and PLAY. Mixed them up, but cover all the Ps for each period. Continue until the family is at PEACE with the budgeted results even if there is little leftover.

The budget is sufficient when there is enough for the whole family. If there are some leftovers, remember to thank your higher power. Increase your expense amount as your income increases to regulate the budget. Please understand that you are only given so many PENNIES every pay period. You as the head of the family must decide how the PENNIES will be divided during each period. Some folks will have 100 PENNIES, while others will have 10,000 to manage. The point to remember is not to compare your PENNIES to another family unit. You ought to take what you have and spread them among your obligations. If by chance you need more PENNIES to manage your household, then your PAY needs to be higher to match what your family requires. For example, if your family members require 1,000 PENNIES per pay period, then you will need sufficient income to balance the budget. Do not purchase anything without first allocating the income to meet your basic needs. After all is done and the budget is set, spread the good word for all you have accomplished to those who want to hear.

If by chance you feel that **you do not have enough income to cover the expenses adequately**, then you must resolve this promptly. Either increase the income or reduce the expenses. Look at all of your expenses and ask yourself the question, do you really need this expense item? If you do not, eliminate or reduce that expense. If you do need the expense, then consider taking on some more income such as a second job, working overtime, etc. I am not suggesting that you do these things if you do not have to. I am recommending that you consider something, especially if you feel that you need to live on more PENNIES than the total income earned by all family members in the household.

Finally, if you do have some leftovers, then I recommend saving them. Remember those PENNIES can be stored, saved for the future. When you plan your budget, take note on how much you need to save for each pay period. If you do not need some of the pennies, then store them in a safe place such as a bank so that you will not be tempted to use them up. Sometimes, out of sight is out of mind. Just make sure that the pennies are far, far out of your arms' reach for safe keeping. Please bear in mind that you will never know when you may get an unexpected visitor and you need to be able to pull out some extra money. It is good to have the extra funds for the unexpected and sometimes unwelcomed guests called emergencies.

Once you have worked through and finalized your P- process at least for the time being, you are now able to sit down and enjoy your free time with ease. Reflect on the goodness of the family coming together and savoring on that well-balanced budget. Finish up your time by taking pleasure on those PENNIES that long ago were so easily spent. If you are blessed to have some remaining at the end of the period – that is great. If not, make every effort to follow your budget by appreciating the Ps given to you. Spread it out as long as you can. Again, do not consume the whole pay check in one sitting. Just start off by dividing up the Ps for the period you are working with, then stretched them as much as you can with a main focus on praying, planning, paying and playing. Get your full-worth – your money's worth. Bon Appetite!

Process 7: Pennies/Peas in a Pot. Keep your pot full.

CHAPTER Q –
Quiz to spend

The quiz is a 10-step process and the results will be recorded at Appendix: Spending ID Card with instructions. This is required by the family in order to obtain your spending license; the quiz must be taken every six months. This test is necessary to be able to lay-out your spending foundation and to develop a plan on how your family will balance total household income. This will be your personal quiz. This is a skill that you will learn through financial preparation, reviewing and practicing by the instructions noted in this book. The final exam is taken periodically; the passing grade is based on how much money you have left-over. You, your spouse and your dependents will set the A-B-C grade scale that's pleasing to the whole family unit.

You do not need a degree in the business field. It is just like brushing your teeth; you do not need to be a dentist to be able to brush your teeth. Similarly, you do not need to be a budget analyst to be able to create your own budget. So, let's get started; now, sharpen your pencils.

1. Compute your ending balance of CASH – this will be your beginning:

The first thing you must do is calculate exactly how much cash you now have. This is considered reconciling all your cash accounts. Add up all the money you have in the house, at the bank (after deducting outstanding checks), non-retirement accounts, etc. This is called your cash-on-hand. Do not count money loaned out, even when the person promises to pay you back soon. Only count the cash you have in your hands (your left hand as well as your right). Once you have a total amount, write in the date as this will be your NEW beginning. Do not spend the money - just recognize it as your balance going forward. Now, you are ready to move forward with a positive beginning.

- ❖ Cash in the house ____________
- ❖ Cash in the checking ____________
- ❖ Cash in the savings ____________
- ❖ Cash in other non-retirement accounts ____________
- ❖ Cash in purse or wallet ____________
- ❖ Cash in some hide away ____________
- ❖ Cash in the jar or piggy bank ____________
- ❖ Other cash ____________

Total – New Beginning (date: ___/___/___) ____________

Note: This information is confidential; please store the completed document in a safe place only to be reviewed by the parties the budget are intended for and no one else.

2. Gather all your financial records and information

This is a major step, please don't skip this step. Pull out the following documents and have them available as needed:

- ❖ Last year's tax return
- ❖ Check book
- ❖ Bank Statements (last 12 months)
- ❖ Pay-stubs and check-stubs (12 months worth)
- ❖ W2s and 1099-MISC Income
- ❖ Business Financial Statements
- ❖ Governmental agency's summary statement
- ❖ Other records showing income

3. Calculate how big your income is monthly.

Now-a-days, some of us have two and three jobs in order to survive. Some folks are living off their renter's income, while others are living off of alimony. As long as it is legal, we all must do what's necessary to meet our needs and some of our wants. Okay let's pull out that calculator; everything needs to be converted into how much "bread" we bring home monthly.

Your income is the foundation to a sound proof budget. This step is critical. You must be thorough and precise or your "slab" will not be solid and your budget will not stand – it will flop.

List your income by the monthly amount; some computing may be needed. If the income category is a yearly amount, then divide the amount by 12. If you are paid weekly, then multiply by 52 then divide by 12. If you are paid twice a month, then multiply the amount by 2 to get your total. If you are paid every other week, that is 26 times a year, then multiply the amount by 26 and then divide by 12. Please follow the examples below to figure the steps to get a precise monthly income amount.

Income Amount	How often paid	Computation	Final Monthly Amount
$60,000	yearly	60000/12	$5,000
$1,000	weekly	1000 X 52 / 12	$4,333
$2,500	twice a month	2500 X 2	$5,000
$2,000	every other week	2000 X 26 / 12	$4,333

For statements such as W2s of which show the gross amount, taxes withheld, insurance cost, and ending with a net amount, use the net amount for simplification purposes. You may change your withholdings later. Review the "tax" chapter later, but right now strictly focus on the budget. From your pay-stub and summary statements, show how much you normally bring in on a monthly basis.

If your pay is different every month, then you must take an average amount. This can be done by adding several months together then dividing by that same number of months. You may want to use your bank statement and/or checkbook to get the information that you need. For example, if you are a salesman and your pay is based on "commissions only" then take an average based on prior history's data. If you are new at selling or this sales period is worse than the prior period, try to project what you expect to bring home based on your professional comfort level and/or the buyer's climate you are working in. As your take-home pay may fluctuate up/down, you may need to adjust your income and budget quarterly.

Make sure that you review your bank statements, summary statements, pay-stubs, checkbook and tax return to ensure that you have considered everything.

Note: This is a family adventure; all income within your household must be included to compute the budget.

Here are some areas to consider when computing income: (Add lines as needed)

- ❖ All Job(s) ________________
- ❖ Personal Business Co. – Schedule C ________________
- ❖ Alimony – only consider if regular ________________
- ❖ Retirement Fund ________________
- ❖ Social Security Income ________________
- ❖ Unemployment Income ________________
- ❖ Governmental Assistance ________________
- ❖ Other income (such as rental property…) ________________

4. Write down total expenses spent last year – code them X, Y, or Z:

X – Means to be deleted
Y – Means to be reduced
Z – Means to be kept as needed

5. Draw a PIE with 10 slices – compute percentages for each slice: This step is necessary as you will compute a before and after snap shot of your expenses. How are your expenses sliced? What is the percentage spent by category? The pie will provide a visual outlook.

- ❖ Charitable Gifts
- ❖ Savings
- ❖ Housing
- ❖ Utilities
- ❖ Food
- ❖ Transportation
- ❖ Children and Pets
- ❖ Medical/Health
- ❖ Personal/Recreation
- ❖ Debt (such as student loans, credit card, etc.)

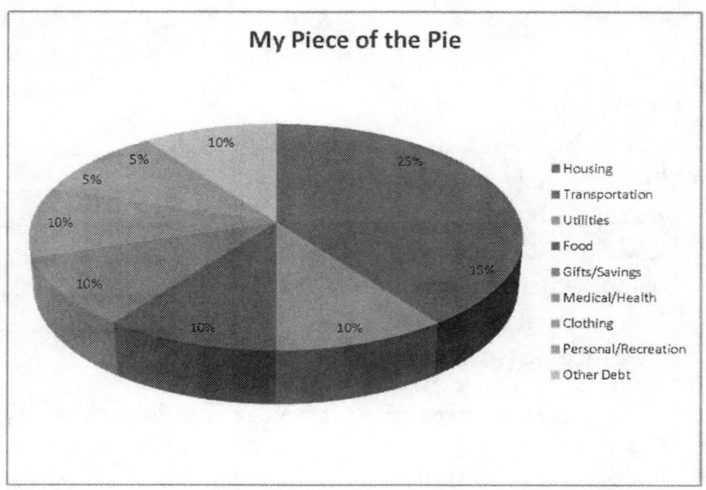

Process 8: Author's Personal Pie

A blank pie is located at Appendix: A Piece of the Pie. Redraw your lines as needed.

6. Schedule a family meeting to discuss the expenses before finalizing the budget.

- Decide which expenses will be eliminated and/or reduced.
- Establish ground rules – for example, when will the family be able to use the credit card.
- Implement a family spending system – such as, the allowance will be distributed consistently on a certain day of the week, the maximum amount to be carried at a given time, etc.
- Discuss how each member will be strong and supportive of this new process.

7. Finally, determine what's important – list them here!

- Maintaining some family time
- Working towards personal dreams
- Spending in order to live comfortably and not to impress others
- Ensuring that the family's values are straight

8. Calculate total expenses less the family's expected allowance – Draft 1.

- See list of detailed expenses at Chapter E.
- See blank budget sheet at Appendix: Income & Expense Budget Sheets.
- See spending license at Appendix: The Spending ID Card with instructions.

9. Work out the budget on paper – balance your budget:

- Charitable Gifts
- Savings
- Housing
- Utilities
- Food
- Transportation
- Children and Pets
- Medical/Health
- Personal/Recreation
- Debt (such as student loans, credit card, etc.)

10. Compute your allowance from what's leftover and select your first grade level.

- Grade and Class A – everyone is ecstatic with their allowance and the budget will easily be met.
- Grade and Class B – everyone is just okay with their allowance; nevertheless the budget will still be met.
- Grade and Class C – some are not O.K. with their allowance; but with some struggle, the budget will still be met.
- Grade and Class D – some are unhappy with their allowance and not very hopeful based on past experience. However, the family is willing to put in the effort necessary so that the budget is met.
- Grade and Class E – everyone is unhappy, because their allowance has been minimized to the bare necessities. Also, the family feels hopeless to meeting the budget. There are some financial challenges and individual issues. Nevertheless, the family is willing to work through the process to balance the budget.

- Grade and Class F – everyone is extremely unhappy, because they have NO allowance – at least for 6 months. There is NO hope that the family will meet the budget. The family feels that there are too many financial challenges and personal issues. The head of the family must stress that this is not the point to give up. Undoubtedly, the family will work through the budget and review/ update every quarter as needed.

Write your allowance and grade on your spending ID card. See picture ID at Appendix: The Spending ID Card with instructions.

A NICE LEFT OVER $XXX.XX

Some Things to Remember

1. The budget should be workable and flexible. Try to experiment with obtaining less expensive items in place of top of the line purchases. If for instance your rent is very high, consider moving. Reduce your expenses to only what you really, really need. Always, be on the lookout for ways to reduce the expenses that you must spend on a purchase – remember timing is everything. Also, note that production cost, overhead and brand name can add to the cost of an item; consider your options.
2. Do not spend unless you have the money to spend. Do not pull out that debit card or write that check if you do not have the funds. Also, set up some policy rules for use of the credit cards as well.
3. Take time out to document every expense item. Keep receipts for every purchase. When using a debit card, maintain the receipt and make notations on them for future reference.
4. Deal only with business folks who are willing to negotiate, because everything is negotiable. Believe me when I say this!
5. Plan for unexpected events to cost you extra; have some extra funds for those types of events. When dealing with an emergency, don't allow the lacking of funds add to the stress level.

CHAPTER R –

Release the old; build a road map.

What is your path? Do you have some direction? Are you moving forward or are you standing still? Are you going in the direction of failure or leading towards success? This is the chapter to assist you in releasing the old map that's leading you towards a dead end and drawing a new map towards a pre-determined financially successful destination.

Before setting out on your new journey, here are the beginning steps to take:

Process 9: A Fork in the Road

1. Dream of where you want to be and what you want to have.
2. Gas up for the long haul. Charge up your GPS – **G**as up with a **P**urposeful **S**avings plan.
3. Ensure that your gears are in working order. SAVE. S=sacrifice; A=advance; V=visualize and victory; E=excel or excellence.
4. Sketch out time for rest stops.
5. Plan for the unexpected bumps & detours in life.
6. Focus on the prize – the final destination.

Before you jump into the driver's seat, you must check out or decide on the following:

1. Set your spending limit for the mission trip.
2. Get rid of the bad oil – lose the debt honestly and diligently.
3. Discuss with family how the steering wheel will be controlled so that the finances won't control you.
4. Keep the tank half full. Don't allow yourself to run low on cash.
5. Maintain a spare: obtain credit or capital as a backup.

6. Make sure you have a first aid kit (budget sheet, calculator and pencil with an eraser).
7. Obtain a gage to ensure that the budget is balanced.
8. Decide on your direction.

What is your path to meet your dreams – set some direction!
In order to make a change in your life, you must have direction. Every individual has a purpose in life. Once you realize your purpose, you can now set your path. Well, in order to get where you are going, you need some funds, in other words you need money. Now that you have direction in your life, you can no longer spend your money on just anything that is not in the path of your dreams. For example, if your dream is to open and run a restaurant, you cannot spend money on material things that you do not need or items that are non-useful for your purpose. This is considered wasteful and you do not have the time nor the money to waste. Now, you must think as if you are already an owner of this business. You need a building for the restaurant, you need top-notch cooking equipment, you need insurance and all items cost money. Your goal now is to obtain sufficient funds to open and run your dream restaurant. So, why would you spend money on items that are not in the direction of your dream? Of course, in running a restaurant, you would not shop for these purchases all at once. You would start by taking baby steps, walking slowly and not running, but more importantly, you must stay focused. The financially stable individuals are the ones aware of their purpose(s) and they are constantly keeping their eyes on that prize. Now, let's take a moment (close your eyes) and dream; think about what you want to do or what you want to have in life. Write those dreams down and work towards that final destination. Review the map – but you must fill in the gap! Turn back to Chapter G to refresh on the "Dream to fruition" process.

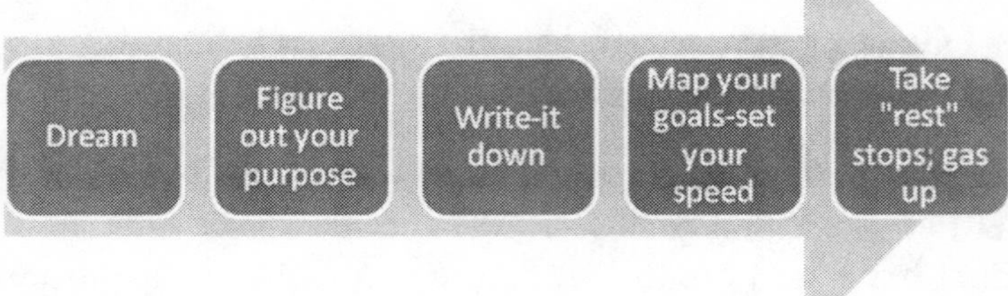

Process 10: Dream to fruition

Remember that when you set up a dream it must be of non-monetary value. I would not recommend that you have a goal of winning, for example, $1,000,000 dollars. The dream should be what you would do with one million dollars. The dream can be anything but money; it can be something that you can touch or something that you can reach. Choose something that is of a non-cash basis; however, the dream can be tangible as well as intangible. If your dream is to win $1,000,000 and you do not have direction once you win the funds, you will spend all of your winnings and you will not have anything to show for it. Dream of the things that you would like to have…now go ahead dream big and see yourself accomplishing those dreams. Write them down and set a path. Say the dream(s) out loud. Now, how does it feel to hear yourself shouting out your goals and/or aspirations? Does it seem real? Do you think that your dreams are assessible? Are you willing to sacrifice some things to reach the goals that you really want? Okay, now it's time to get that map out and set your own path. But first, let's look at a few sample wants:

a. To buy a house or buy a bigger house
b. To start a business or expand the current business
c. To send the children to college (debt-free); to complete your college degree
d. To travel to Australia or another country with the family
e. To assist in the cure of hypertension; contribute one year of your time for the cause without the concern of your personal expenses
f. To retire early and take up a new hobby

Now it is time to map your path. I will use the first example to show you how to map out your dreams. Try to visualize the steps.

1. My starting point is to move from a 3-bedroom house to a 5-bedroom with 2 1/2 bathroom mansion. I plan to head South to be close to family.
2. Turn left onto "Pay off debt" lane. This will take 3.3 years. I am willing to sacrifice by reducing my spending on clothing that I do not need. The adjusted time to get to the next stop is 2.6 years.
3. Turn right onto "Saving for down-payment" Cove. This will take 8 months. I have extra income since I have paid down my debt.
4. I just found out that I need an operation; I must take a detour and merge onto "Wait another year" circle until I am able to return to work and recoup the loss of income.
5. Now, I am back on the expressway and I am ready to take "I have found my dream house" avenue.
6. Before moving forward, I must first rest to pay some bills that have come due. I have estimated that I need two months to get caught up again. I have decided that I do not want to move into a new house without being able to buy a new dining room table. Plan to set the funds aside to make this happen by the move-in date.
7. It's Christmas time, and normally I spend a great deal to please everyone in the family, but I am focused. My eyes are on the prize – getting that brand new (and bigger) house.
8. I must pull over onto "almost there" street, because I need to gas up. My cash is low but I have improved my credit and soon I will have that capital (house) that I dreamed about owning. I need another four months.
9. GPS has instructed me to back up and turn Right onto "must sign all those papers" highway. I have stayed within my budget, I am in balance and I am on target.
10. Finally, I take the ramp to "Home Sweet Home" to live there for the next 15 years or so.

Comments: This trip took approximately five years. <u>There was one detour</u>, but I did not let the major event deter me from accomplishing my dream. Each map would have various steps, time slots for each step and funds needed to complete each step. At the end of the road, write down the total time and funds required to reach that next destination. Lastly, once you have reached that dream spot, take a rest stop and then move on to the next dream spot. As long as you are living, you should continue to dream. Now, take a moment and dream. Summarize your dream at Appendix: My Personal Financial Contracts.

CHAPTER S –
Save, Save, Save!!!

It is extremely difficult to save when you need every bit of your funds just to pay the basic expenses. Also, I realize there is no incentive to save when the banks are not even providing at least 1% interest for you to be willing to deposit your hard earned money into a savings account. There are some options, but make sure that your funds are protected by FDIC (federally insured). This means that your funds, up to $250,000 are safe even if the bank goes under and shuts down. Visit the financial institutions that offer more than 1% interest on your deposited funds. Ask about their high-yield savings accounts and/or their money market accounts. This may be something to look into even though there may be some restrictions. Also, if you are comfortable with the internet, there are some banks authorized to operate via on-line ONLY where you can transact banking business and open an on-line savings account. There is no building to go to; everything is conducted on-line. These types of institutions are able to save on overhead costs. Therefore, they are able to provide a larger interest return on your savings account. Make sure that you do your research to ensure your funds are safe, easily accessible and insured by the federal government. Wherever you decide to go locally or internationally, I strongly urge you to open and maintain some type of savings account and save as much as your budget allows.

Here are the reasons why you need to save:

- ✓ Save for a rainy day. (to repair or fix the mishaps). - Tier I
- ✓ Save for an emergency. (to cover the unexpected). - Tier II
- ✓ Set aside a reserve. (three-six months expenses). - Tier III
- ✓ Set aside funds for college. - Tier IV
- ✓ Invest in a retirement plan. - Tier V
- ✓ Set aside an extra amount for the luxuries in life. - Tier VI

There are six tiers to saving. If you are able, I would recommend saving a percentage of your income at each tier. Start off saving by setting aside part of your income check until you have reached $1,000 in Tier I, then move to Tier II and save until you have reached the minimum amount of $5,000. Continue to move up the tiers until you have reached your goal at each tier. Notice that the "retirement" tier is Tier V. This does not mean that you have to wait until you have completed the other tiers before you start with Tier V. Maybe if you have 10 cents to save, you may want to save half of it for Tier V. It takes many, many years to build up your retirement fund and the sooner you start the better. To keep track and to separate the savings' tier categories, I would suggest setting up a separate savings account for each tier. This is very important so that when you need to pull funds from a particular area, you will be able to keep track of the remaining funds by the account category. Also, when you use funds from a particular account, you must replenish the money as quickly as possible.

In my personal situation, I had been unemployed for over a year, I had to pull funds from each of my accounts except for my retirement fund. I maintained my retirement account because I knew that I would be taxed dearly if I dipped into that account. I have not yet reached that magic number: 59 ½ years old. Also, when you are unemployed, there are no luxuries, just surviving. Oh course; I was not focused on the income taxes nor the luxuries. When I received that full-time job, I will begin again to save by starting over at Tier 1. Do not be upset with life's challenges that will cross your path; be thankful that you will have the funds to cover until the storm passes over. This is why you have the funds; now you are able to relax.

Be careful not to use the funds set aside for unexpected events to take part in a department store sale for an outfit you feel that you must have. Is this truly an emergency? At the start of saving, I suggest that you document a "when to…" plan. There are two procedures that you must document:

- A savings plan
- A savings policy

A savings plan provides detailed information to the family on where the funds will come from. Here are some examples:

- You may have recently stopped smoking those 2 packs of cigarettes daily. You plan to use the savings for Tier I & II equally. The money that was used to purchase a case of cigarettes will now go into the Tier I & Tier II accounts.

- Currently you decided to cut back on going out to eat. The savings will go towards Tier III. The family used to eat out at least 3 times a week. Now, the family can set aside funds in a reserve account. This is just in case one is laid off or gets sick, and needs the funds to survive for a given time period.
- With internet access, the family feels there is no need for cable television. The savings will go towards the children's college fund. This represents Tier IV.

Of course, the family jointly would decide what areas they are willing to eliminate, cut back or stop to be able to save the necessary funds for the unexpected and expected events that may cross the family's path.

A savings policy should be documented to provide the details on why you are saving and what is the particular goal. The policy is short, sweet and to the point. It is a guide for the "what ifs" in life. Here is an example:

> *I have deposited $1,000.00 into a separate account that represents Tier 1. The funds will be used for minor automotive repair services and for small fix-ups around the house. This tier will not be used to replace parts and/or furniture that are working properly. This account will be used for mishaps or sudden breakdowns to the car and the house ONLY.*

This must be completed for each Tier. Also, you should consider the process of obtaining the funds as needed. When you have a sudden breakdown, how will you pull out the funds? If you were to write a check for the payment, you can transfer the needed amount from the appropriate tier account to the checking account. If you were to pay by credit card, then pay off the balance (once the bill arrives) by using the funds from the tier account.

Remember, once the savings' goals have been reached, the family will discuss new ones. Here are the steps (questions) to be answered under the savings plan. Each tier is a separate goal (dream) that the family needs to agree upon and write.

1. What is the initial amount you are willing to invest?
2. How much are you willing to deposit on a routine basis?
3. How frequent will you make the agreed upon deposit?
4. What is the expected time frame to reach the savings plan goal?

For example, maybe you plan to save $1,000 for a rainy day within a year. Provided below is how to write up the savings plan and how to implement the rainy day objective:

<u>Savings Plan for Tier I</u>
Initial amount: $100.00
Deposit amount: $ 20.00
Frequency level: weekly
Expected Time: 46 weeks
Computation: $100 + ($20 times 45 weeks) =
$100 + $900 = $1,000

It's that plain and simple. Now you try it; start with just one goal (step) at a time:

<u>Savings Plan for Tier I</u>
Initial amount: $__________
Deposit amount: $__________
Frequency level: daily or weekly or monthly (circle one)
Expected Time: ________ weeks or months or years (circle one)
Computation: initial amount + (deposit amount X frequency#)

Equation 1: Savings Plan Computation

Well, you may be closer to reaching your goal than you think. Put up as little as $10.00 or as much as you feasibly can handle on a regular basis until you have saved up what you may need in your life. Now, you can do it. Why not start today.

I have provided some additional detail so that you are able to recognize how and when the funds saved are to be used. The definition of each tier is agreed upon by the family.

For my family, **<u>TIER I</u>** is when the car breaks down or when there is a flat tire. The tires on my car cost around $300. The decision was made to have $800 in the Tier I account.

<u>TIER II</u> is when someone in the family gets sick and the person needs an operation. The family's deductible is $2,000 for over-night operations. Tier II is set up for this type of emergency. You may use Tier II for some other type of emergency such as the roof craving in due to a bad storm that hit the area. If you do not have the insurance coverage to replace the roof as you may so desperately need, then Tier II is set up for this type of emergency. Please note that we all will have some type of emergency in our life time. The question is how do you handle the emergencies in your life? Do you have extra funds or will you have to borrow the needed funds? It is so nice when all you have to do is write a check to cover the "break downs" that could set you back if you don't have what you need financially.

TIER III is for lay-offs from the main source of income. The guessing game is how long will you be without a job and how much will you need to survive? The funds that you are able to set aside may never be used, but if you are released from employment, this reserve account is a great thing to have. Yes, I had 6 months worth of my salary in a reserve account, but I was unemployed for over two years. Who would have thought that I needed two years worth of my salary set aside? Well, something is better than nothing. I was able to stretch my money out for 12 months with grace by sacrificing a great deal until I was able to enjoy employment again.

TIERS IV and V are provided for my daughter who wants to attend college and for me who wants to live comfortably during the retirement years. I do not plan to depend on the government to provide for the things that I want in life.

The final **TIER VI** is for the luxuries in life. If you like to travel, you may want to set up a vacation fund to cover the yearly trips that you want to take with the family. Some individuals use this tier to set up a Christmas fund so that they are able to buy lavish gifts for close family members and friends without going into debt.

Save as much as you can. At least 3 to 6 months of your salary should be set aside for the unexpected, such as loss of a close family member, loss of a job, major home repairs, and the list goes on and on and on. Anything could happen and the last thing you want to be concerned with are your finances. So, please start now. Just do it!!! This is your safety net: your family may not be able to help, the government may be lacking, and the loan institutions may be too costly. This is your life; now build your own safety net and save.

CHAPTER T –
Stop focusing on the taxes

Stop spending a great deal of your time focusing on federal, state and local taxes. A taxing of the people has been going on since the beginning of time. Taxation is mentioned numerous times in the King James Version of the Bible. It was first mentioned in the command (Ex. 30:11-16) that every Jew from twenty years and upward should pay an annual tax of "half a shekel for an offering to the Lord." This enactment was faithfully observed for many generations. Also, the Bible discusses that you pay taxes for civil purposes. Not much has changed over the centuries, now you pay taxes because it's your civic duty.

Listed are several scriptures noting taxation of the people and their land:

I Kings 4:7...each man his month in a year made <u>provision</u>...

I Kings 9:15...and this is the reason of the <u>levy</u>...for to build the house of the Lord...

II Kings 12:4...all the <u>money</u> of the dedicated things that is brought into the house of the Lord, even the <u>money</u> of every one that passeth the account, the <u>money</u> that every man is set at, and all the money that cometh into any man's heart to bring into the house of the Lord.

II Kings 23:35...but he <u>taxed</u> the land to give the <u>money</u> according to the commandment...

II Chronicles 24:5...Go out unto the cities of Judah, and gather of all Israel <u>money</u> to repair the house of your God from year to year...

II Chronicles 24:6...Why hast thou not required of the Levites to bring in out of Judah and out of Jerusalem the <u>collection</u>, according to the commandment of Moses...

Daniel 11:20...then shall stand up in his estate a raiser of <u>taxes</u> in the glory of the kingdom...

Matthew 17:24…they that received tribute money came to Peter, and said, Doth not your master pay tribute…

Luke 2:1-5…that all the world should be taxed…every one into his own city…and Joseph also went up from Galilee…to be taxed with Mary his espoused wife, being great with child…

Acts 5:37…in the days of the taxing…

Currently, we have the Internal Revenue Code that discusses income taxes of Income, Estate, Gifts, Employment and Excise Taxes, just to name a few. There are two volumes with approximately 10,000 sections recorded. We call our tax man – Uncle Sam. Accept it as fact, the United States will forever charge against a citizen's person, property and activity for the support of the government. Please recognize that taxation is a part of life, so let's acknowledge it, accept it, pay it and just move on.

The next thing to recognize is that if it is income to you then most likely it's taxable for the government. When you are taxed, the assessment is income for the government. This chapter is not to educate you on the various tax codes and laws; it's written to help you understand that taxation is here to stay. I do not want you to focus on how to get out of paying taxes; I want you to focus on the bigger picture: making money, budgeting money, saving money and investing money. Through the in-flow of money, you will be taxed. This is okay because in the end, you will have sufficient funds to cover your obligations and responsibilities which include your expense of income taxes. The operative word here is ***sufficient funds***. That is the focus of this book as well as in this chapter.

With that in mind, pay your taxes and pay them on time. Avoid by all means possible any interest fees and penalties. Communicate with the government, as much as humanly feasible, when you cannot pay your tax bill in full. Consult with a tax professional on how you should make those partial payments.

Of course, I will advise you not to cheat on your taxes, but to legally take advantage of all deductions, credits and exemptions. If you qualified for any deductions and/or credits, by all means take them. If you are exempt from paying taxes, do not feel left out. You are only obligated to pay what you owe.

Finally, do not live your life around your income taxes. For example, do not obtain a 2nd mortgage just to take advantage of the interest deductions. I need you to realize that what is tax law today may not be an option the following year. Case-in-point, once upon a time you were able to deduct credit card interest expenses on your federal tax return. Folks would charge up their credit cards, did not pay them off to rack up on interest expense in order to get that tax deduction. When the law was changed in 1986, it devastated a significant number of tax payers because now they had the interest expense but no tax deduction. Americans were (and now) addicted to using credit to make major as well as minor purchases. Some are still paying for years of bad choices made regarding building up interest charges that are no longer deductible. Live your life as a law binding citizen, spend within your budget and if you able to take a tax deduction, take it and run.

Now, when I share with you how to make extra money from your own money by way of interest income or dividend income, I want you to do it and be proud of the amount that you have made. Do not ever mention that you are frustrated that you have to pay taxes on the interest income that you made during the year. Pay your taxes and be proud of the fact that you can.

CHAPTER U –
Are you Uninsured or Underinsured?

Are you uninsured or underinsured? Uninsured is not having insurance when you really need it. Underinsured is not having enough insurance. Read this chapter carefully in order to obtain just enough knowledge to feel assured that you and your family are purchasing sufficient insurance to meet your financial needs as well as your personal needs.

Everyone wants to feel secure and basic insurance coverage for the family is just like a security blanket for a child who is extremely shy. The child is reassured that no one will bother him/her if he/she has that blanket. Well, insurance is just that: protection against possible future loss. Unlike the security blanket, insurance does not protect you against obtaining the loss; it covers you after the loss. It is similar to an umbrella in the rain. You cannot stop the rain from pouring down, but you can cover yourself from getting drenched. Now, the question is how "wet" are you willing to get? The level of wetness you are willing to get will help you to decide how much insurance to purchase. If you do not purchase the adequate amount of insurance then you are considered to be "underinsured." To be underinsured could be just as bad as being uninsured. When the need arises, the insurance company may not be able to cover you. If you are not covered, you will pay dearly.

To protect your family and assets through general insurance is the act of insuring, or assuring, against loss or damage due to a subsequent event. A contract is signed with an agreed upon stipulated & financial consideration for the consequent loss. The cost or premium of the insurance depends on the risk level. The risk is the predicted occurrence level of an adverse event. With regard to insurance, it is the chance for the loss or damage to occur.

There are four types of risk:

1. High risk – for example, the risk of getting cancer.
2. Blind risk – for example, the risk of getting into a car accident.
3. Diminish risk – the risk of preventive treatments through health insurance.
4. Level risk – the risk to maintain comfort…the need for long term health-care.

To determine the level of insurance that the family needs will take careful risk analysis based on the family's current circumstances. Also, to feel confident that you have sufficient coverage and not wait until the aftermath of a major accident, property damage, individual sickness or even death, you must consider the gaps, caps and exclusions. A **gap** is the difference between the amount of money you have and the amount you will need to provide for the potential loss. For example, if you have $5,000 savings to be used as insurance to cover the cost of a funeral and the costs are projected to be around $12,000; the gap is $7,000. You will need some type of life insurance to cover the gap. The **cap** is the maximum amount that an insurance company (or insurer) will undertake for a particular policy plan. For example, if the liability coverage under your automobile insurance is $500,000 per accident, then the maximum that the insurance company will cover for bodily injury, pain and suffering, medical bills, funerals, lost income and property damage to the other car is the cap of $500,000. The **exclusion** is the insurance coverage plan that explicitly excludes certain provisions from the contract. Let's say that you have homeowners' insurance and it covers the following:

- Fire or lightning
- Windstorm or hail
- Explosion
- Riot or civil disturbance
- Damage from an aircraft
- Damage from a vehicle
- Smoke damage
- Vandalism or malicious mischief
- Theft
- Breakage of glass that is part of a building
- Volcanic eruption

The following perils may be excluded from the homeowners' contract:

- Flood
- Earthquake
- War
- Nuclear accident

If the risk level of a flood occurring in your community is high then you ought to make sure that you have homeowners' (or rentals') insurance to cover just in case a major storm were to hit your neighborhood. Recently in Memphis, Tennessee, a major flood resulted after several severe storms hit the town, many families lost their homes. Be aware of the terminology, "flood" as it is used in your insurance policy. As an inclusion of flood in the policy, does it pertain to a flood as a result of your washing machine malfunctioning by water overflowing and causing a flood in your house? Or, is the term, "flood" defined as Mother Nature hitting the house, causing a flood and damages to your property? It is crucial, beforehand to check with the insurer to get clarity on the type of insurance you have. Also, you must feel comfortable with whether you have the right type of insurance as well as the right level.

Make sure that you <u>**read the fine print**</u> to ensure that you have a solid safety net. A safety net is something that catches (or covers) you and your family members in order to prevent a mishap from becoming catastrophic. What matters is that you understand your needs, comprehend your options and select the specific insurance plan that meets all of your needs.

So, why do you need insurance? There are three (3) main reasons:

- ✓ To mitigate a severe family crisis.
- ✓ To mitigate potential loss of income.
- ✓ To limit the negative consequences of such events.

Remember the risk is not eliminated but the risk is transferred to the insurer, in most cases this represents the insurance company. Your insurance may be set up where you pay some upfront cost such as a deductible. If, for example, a rock were to hit your windshield on your car and the total cost to replace the glass was $500.00, the deductible is your out-of-pocket cost that you will have to pay before the automobile insurance kicks in. If the deductible is $100.00, then the insurance would cover $400.00. To decide on the amount for your deductible depends on three factors:

- ✓ The risk of the event occurring
- ✓ The cost of changing the deductible amount
- ✓ The amount of personal funding set aside

If the risk of a rock hitting the car is high, in order words, on numerous occasions your car has been hit with rocks, then your risk level is considered high in this example. In addition, the extra cost to include the coverage of flying objects hitting car while driving is nominal to your budget then I would recommend obtaining the coverage. If by chance this coverage was costly and you had the additional personal funds set aside for those types of mishaps, then I would recommend NOT obtaining that type of coverage.

Obtaining insurance is a personal decision. Therefore, this book will not instruct you on what type of insurance to obtain and what type to leave on the table. This book is available to share the essential personal decision making tools that are needed and the factors that need to be considered. Also, it should be your choice on whether to make that move and you should not be influenced by scare tactics from the insurance agent. There are options that you should consider before you sign on the dotted line. Here are four (4) things to consider:

- ➢ The level of risk you are willing to tolerate – "how wet are you willing to get?"
- ➢ The level of risk to be transferred
- ➢ The likelihood of the risk happening
- ➢ The cost (premium) of transferring the risk

There are tons of insurance plans to be considered. There was only one that really surprised me: health insurance on pets. Generally, there are five major types of insurance coverage to choose from. From this list, I recommend that you undertake and identify the coverage needed by developing your own personalized list to provide the financial and emotional well-being that will significantly lower the stress and likelihood of debilitating events that could have on one's life. <u>There is a 100% chance that something unexpectedly will happen in your life.</u> Having the proper amount of insurance just makes the challenges in life more bearable.

Here are the major types of fundamental risks:

- Death
- Disability
- Accident or sickness
- Property loss or damage
- Litigation for negligence

Remember, the main purpose of insurance is to preserve and protect your assets so that you will have something to pass on to your heirs. You want to protect the lifestyle you have struggled to attain for your future as well as for your family's future. Insurance coverage is maintaining and building upon that dynasty; creating a firm foundation for the next generation <u>to move up the financial ladder</u> and leaving behind economic support for the well-being of your children and their children, and so on. To have the proper amount of insurance and to enjoy the benefits is a great plan to have. This may be an important item to add to the objectives list. Just make sure that you formalize a plan to get the insurance you require; review and update your needs yearly.

CHAPTER VW –
Victory to Winning

Victory is a successful ending to a struggle. Winning is succeeding with great difficulty. Also, it is the act of obtaining something special. Now, you can finally say that the battle is almost over. I am sure that you realize that winning is not everything. But when you fight, the fight is not only to end the battle, but the fight is to gain something from all the hard work. So, what is it that you want to gain? Is it money that you are interested in, the green bill, the lean mean **(In God We Trust)** thing, the almighty dollar, the dough, bread, cabbage, shekels, sterling, gold, wealth, coins, hard cash, pocket money, ready money, spending money, small change, currency or even maybe a promissory note will suffice? What do you plan to do with the funds once it is in your possession? Do you plan to bury it, sleep on it, kiss it or keep it until you are dead and gone and request that it is placed close to your bosom? Now, you finally have the answers. You realize that the funds obtained are useless in the "idle" mode. There needs to be a plan in place that shows how the gain will be spent; this must happen before you get the victory and the winnings.

I have met a huge number of wealthy people, folks with an abundance of material possessions and resources. These people were rich and quite affluent. They had a plentiful supply of material goods and money, yet they were very unhappy. At first my thinking was that they had the "winning number." Yet, when I spoke with them, they did not feel victorious. Well, I learned as a teenager from my first work experience at Landmark Bank that financial prosperity in and of itself will not make you happy. We all have a purpose; your purpose may not be just to be wealthy alone, but to complete your mission(s) successfully while here on earth. <u>To bring in the bucks is not sufficient enough; you need a purpose, objectives and direction.</u>

Individuals who have comprehensive or specific goals are happier than the individuals who do not have any goals at all. Setting goals are very important because it provides something for you to look forward to. <u>**When you have money but no goals there is nothing for you to aim for.**</u> Some people think that rich people have it all, but soon they realize that all they have are some dirty, old, and torn up bills. That well-off person has the funds but do not know what to do or where to go if he/she has no goals.

How do you start identifying your financial goals to reach the winning line? You start by thinking about what you hope for or what you want people to say when they think of you? What are your expectations and what do you want to leave behind? Also, you may want to start thinking about your concerns that may financially affect your family? Do you have expense shortfalls or are you lacking in income? This is the best time to set up a financial strategy. This appears to be challenging at first, but it gets easier each time you review and update your strategy.

Here's how to construct your very own personal financial strategy. Begin by listing your financial concerns, necessary life changing events, physical objects to acquire, expectations for the children, dreams for the family, new adventures to complete or just structure a goal to be financially independent. By constructing your personalized list, you are in essence developing your own full financial checkup cheat sheet. A full financial checkup is needed every 6 months. There may be adjustments and/or changes needed, but you have the cheat sheet. You have all of the answers. Therefore, concentrate on what will fill your tank to gain and maintain that ultimate victory to financial independence. These would be all of your accomplishments necessary to feel fulfilled to the upmost highest life expectancy. Are you ready to climb that pyramid?

Recognize that this is a **life-time journey**. You would build your own financial pyramid by starting off the first round fighting for the first phase victory, then going to battle for financial independence, and not stopping until the very end to become the ultimate WINNER. Sometimes you will get tired, sometimes you want to throw in the towel and just quit. **Do not quit!!!** But, every so often you will need to pause or just request a time out. It's okay to pause for a break. Just be brief so that you can get back to work, because you have a purpose and you now know your direction. Start the climb with small baby steps by setting short-term goals to reach the next level which are the in-between goals and finally to those long term goals for life. Short-term goals are usually completed within one year. In-between goals may take one to five years to complete. Long-term goals are major lifestyle events of which will have a huge impact on your finances. These goals should take five years or more to accomplish. When one goal is complete, then initiate the next set of goals. If you are stuck on one goal, then transition over to another goal. You will always have a fight through the various stages. Stay focused on those goals until you have reached the victory of financial independence. Then you can pass go to the end of the line as a winner. When you have reached the top of one pyramid, then start the climb of yet another one. **Continue to climb** until your journey on earth is complete.

Process 11: From victory to winning

CHAPTER X –

X out the negatives!!!

Those who wish to sing, always find a song. - Swedish Proverb

Those who dream to be wealthy will always have great wealth. – Cynthia's Proverb

Equation 2: Dream Proverb

X – Get rid of those negative people, places, things and ideas. Also, eliminate those negative words. Never react from a negative statement or thought. Release the negative and replace with positive phrases. Can you become wealthy – yes, you can.

Are you curious to know why such a chapter would be in a finance book? Well, negativity can hold you back in most areas, especially in finances. If you are negative, you will miss some great opportunities. Let's repeat the ABCs now. Your attitude, your family's beliefs, your friend's characteristics, the places you hang out, the things you possessed and the ideas roaming around in your head have a great effect on how you manage your money. You will gamble away huge amounts based on the negative aroma released around you. When I say gamble, I am not just talking about gambling at the casino. You can gamble away your funds at the stores, on the internet or by the telephone. The negativity around you can cause you to take big risks or no risks at all. *Due to your negative surroundings, you may not think your decisions through when it comes to purchasing an item, signing a contract, quitting a job, overlooking a better opportunity and the list goes on and on and on.* Would you believe that such a concept could have an unconstructive, show stopping, constricting strong grip on such an intelligent individual like yourself? Therefore, you must release all the negative people, places, things and ideas immediately.

Negativity can affect the quality of your life. With negativity, you will lack the confidence to negotiate the finances for a product that you desire to have. You would settle for less than you deserve and you will not push yourself to achieve. You'll accept a mediocre, dull life because you'll assume you don't deserve anything else. And, more importantly, you will worry a lot about what others think of you and this will additionally hamper you in pursuing your dreams. You will not be willing to take some calculated risks. If you are around negative people, you cannot be successful. Negative people are seen as jealous in a begrudging manner and they are all too quick to throw insults. They are constantly telling you that you are crazy and the positive things will never happen to you. You cannot associate with people that are negative. Also, the negative places that you grace yourself do not correlate with people trying to make an effort to change their lives for the better. Sometimes, the negativity comes from outside sources and sometime it comes from within. It is extremely important not to listen and follow those negative thoughts flowing through and around your head regarding life and financial matters. You have to constantly work at controlling what you hear as well as controlling how you react to what you have heard.

If at all possible, limit your time spent with people who are negative and who say negative things to you. First of all, you do not have the time and secondly, you have goals to be accomplished. Remember when a negative object (that is, person, place, thing or idea) comes into close proximity... make a quick exit.

No one has the right to insult or belittle you. The less time you spend with such people, the better off you will feel. And, the better you feel, the more time you have to start pursuing your dreams. Negative words affect our self-image, so start to change the words you use, picking positive words instead of negative ones. Try not to start a sentence with...always or never, such as I will ***never*** accomplish my dreams or I will ***always*** be poor. With practice, this will become easier and you will soon reap the rewards of increased confidence and higher self-esteem. You will also be better equipped to deal with negative people and their negative words. You will begin to feel rather sorry for them and wish that they too could realize that negative words affect them greatly and thus begin to change their ways and become more positive. ***The bottom line is that you must protect yourself from any negativity that comes in your midst.***

When you cease to poison your mind with negative words you will notice that you will feel lighter in spirit, happier and more generous to those around you. You'll no longer see problems, only opportunities. You won't complain as much or focus on anything negative or bad. You will recognize that you are too busy thinking positive thoughts and pursuing your ambitions and dreams.

Here are some crippling effects on negativity. Negativity can:

- Keep you from enjoying what you have; you are constantly buying stuff to make yourself happy.
- Keep you from trying new things or doing things differently that may turn out to be just wonderful.
- Keep you from learning how to cope with the challenges of life, such as unemployment, sickness, increased prices, etc.
- Keep you and the people around you from being happy and objects cannot satisfy you.
- Allow you to give up on a situation quickly. Unable to think of other possible alternatives.
- Take away your energy and motivation. You lose that go-get-them attitude.
- Make you critical, cynical , skeptical, suspicious, untrusting and greedy. With greed, your thoughts are confused on what you want with how you will go about getting what you want.
- Make you think like a child…pure irrational and immature process thinking.
- Make you feel helpless with no positive hope for the future.
- Strip you from maximizing your full potential and God's purpose.

From a physical standpoint, negativity, unhappiness, and stress will weaken your immune system. When this happens, you can become susceptible to many diseases, such as heart disease, ulcers, other pains and ailments. And, when you are sick, you do not have the strength to work towards that great wealth that you so desire and deserve.

Spend some time meditating on the words noted in the Appendix: Your Pledge to Stop. See the back of the book.

There is hope – stop the negatives:

- Just exit to the left or to the right – you must exit promptly.
- Replace the negative thoughts with something positive.
- Do not react or make a decision on a negative thought.
- Write down the things you are thankful for and review the list periodically.
- Repeat out loud (in the mirror) the things that you are thankful for.

- Focus on the things that make you smile, the things that you appreciate, enjoy and love.
- Write down how a bad situation in your life can be positive; this helps to build character.
- Try not to complain; instead say something positive.
- See the good in everything…people and situations.
- Make an effort to visualize the problems rolling off your back similar to water rolling off a duck's back.
- Work diligently on your attitude from the negative to the positive. Improve your attitude.
- Do not attempt to change the other person's attitude…focus on your own personal goals.

Now, have I sold you on releasing the negativity or do I need to negotiate with you some more?

Comment below on how you will do things differently to release the negativity in your life and to strive for financial independence:

____

____

____

____

____

____

____

____

____

For Immediate Release
Office of the Press Secretary
Family's Proclamation
January 1, 20____

CHAPTER YZ –

Year-round plan; must be followed with zeal

Good financial management takes total commitment, fortitude and involvement from everyone in the family. The family working together by sharing responsibilities is an important value to have as a family unit. Let us highlight the many benefits of budgeting and saving; these utilized tools add value to the family structure. By taking steps to dream, defining goals and completing those goals, the family can enhance its wealth with financial independence and freedom...this is the prosperity that this family has longed for and now it's visible and reachable. First, we must pause to remember and give thanks to the Almighty God for the challenges he has brought us through thus far and what the Almighty will bring us through as we persevere forward.

This day is set forth to recognize the importance of cooperative efforts to work together and to promote unity among the family members within the dwelling. With the preparation of the family's balance sheet, budget sheet, cash flow statement, spending license and the completion thereof, the family will be able to celebrate a milestone and record this in history. The financial advancement of this family is a story book of this time and a new zeal is being written before our very eyes. This family needs to continue to strive and remember the financial alphabet for the good of the household.

NOW, THEREFORE, I, ________________________, the Head of the family, by virtue of the authority vested in me by the ABCs that make cents, the - Peas in the pot, the Bees diminished, do hereby proclaim ___________________ as the beginning of a new path to be reviewed periodically. I call upon all individuals in this household to educate and motivate others by spreading the word (of this book) through various activities and communications on how to carry forward the purpose through financial money management. Today, let us seek God's guidance and His blessings as we press onward to succeed upward given our new direction. Now, it is up to us to carry forth the plan by climbing our financial ladder one step at a time.

IN WITNESS WHEREOF, I have hereunto set my hand this first day of ____________, in the year of our Lord two thousand ____, and of the greatness of this family.

#####Chapter Z-end#####

Summary Chapter of the ABCs to do list

Chapter ABC Attitudes, Behaviors and Characteristics to spending: Write a sentence or two regarding your attitude and behavior towards money. How would you characterize your spending habits? Rate yourself by the following categories:

☐bargainer ☐carefree ☐cautious ☐loose ☐saver

Sub-Chapter A Analyze your family's life style. Observe for a month on how you spend money. Write down what triggers you to spend. Do you spend money as if you were a <u>cash cow</u> or are you a <u>penny pincher</u>? Discuss with a close friend or family member how you plan to manage your triggers and other personal influences in your life.

Sub-Chapter B Buying, Begging, Biting and Borrowing must be diminished. Look at what you are buying and begging for. Ask yourself the following question: do I really need those items? Consider whether or not you are biting more than you can chew and whether you are borrowing too much. Start a plan to diminish those BAD habits.

Sub-Chapter C Cash, Credit and/or Capital – you should have access to at least two out of these three categories. Which of the three other than cash do you prefer? List ways that you can obtain funds and survive in addition to the cash that you have. Write down the capital investments that you have acquired in your name such as your house. Consider your 'credit' options as a backup plan just in case you do not have access to your cash or your cash has been depleted.

Chapter D

How is money delivered to you? Think about how your funds are provided to you. How are you managing the cash received at each pay period? Think about your options and costs. Is there an extra fee to obtain your funds via a debit card? Think about the most effective way to receive your funds. Consider the most efficient and the safest way to pay your routine and budgeted expense items.

Chapter E

Reduce expenses in an effort to eliminating debt. Write down every expense item that you spend your money on. Consider whether the expense is a necessary item. Label your expenses and note whether or not your family falls within the average statistics by income, expense category and size of family.

Chapter F

Your financial affairs should be in order! There is a process to getting your life in financial order. First you must complete a balance sheet showing all of your assets such as your house, car, etc. on one side of the sheet and all of your liabilities such as your mortgage, loans, bills, etc. on the other side. Deduct those liabilities from your assets; this will calculate to be your net-worth. Produce the other needed financial documents and store them in a safe place. Figure out what you are going to do with the items that have a zero or negative net-worth. Set-up a plan and balance your life with your balance sheet so that you can live out your dreams.

Chapter G

Goals are very important. What are your goals? Are you upbeat about them? Okay, <u>start by closing your eyes and dream</u>. Think about what you want to do in life. Now, open your eyes. Write those dreams down and work towards that final "destination". Draw up a map, layout the plan and fill in the gaps! There are three basic steps: determine the goal; determine the cost; and, determine the speed in which you plan to accomplish your goal. When your spirit of accomplishing your goals breaks down, figure out ways to energize yourself back on track. Do not give up; keep striving until your dreams become reality.

Chapter H I The highly valued inventory may be worthless – Look at each item individually. Implement the chapter's process on how to handle a new purchase. First, you would take the product out of the box and put the individual parts together. This is considered your inventory. Once the item is ready to be used, take a picture of that special or unique item and maintain it with the sales receipt and product manual. Store the records in a fireproof safe and/or safe deposit box at a bank. Keep an extra copy of the picture and sales receipt with the inventory worksheet. This may seem cumbersome. Just too much work for just inventory, but after this is completely implemented you will be pleased with the results.

Chapter JKL Just keep level-headed regarding your finances. There are 5 various levels of expenses. Do you know which ones you use the most? Recognize yours as this is the beginning to understanding how to stay level-headed and the ending to not slicing more than you can chew. To maintain balance the family needs to incorporate a budget for everyone's daily use. There are steps to take to set-up a budget; the budget is a positive correlation to level-headedness. Using the budget will help you to stay level-headed. In addition to this chapter, read over Chapter E, to ensure that you have considered all the pertinent expense items in regards to your family. Remove the blank pie chart (located in the Appendix) and use it as a visual aid to assist you in working through the budget. Remember to stay level headed and only use the allotted income given you at each pay period.

Chapter M & N Always monitor your net-worth. Net-worth is the difference between the value of what you own less the value of what you owe. Your net-worth should be positive and never negative. There are ways to increase your net-worth without purchasing more stuff. Realize that there may be one main asset that is bringing down your net-worth. Should you sell that asset? This chapter will show that getting rid of an asset may not improve your net-worth. <u>The best way to increase your net-worth is by decreasing your debt.</u> Do not feel depress if you cannot pay off your debt right away. Nevertheless, you ought to devise a plan of action. "My Personal Payoff Contract" and "The Debt Schedule" are provided in the Appendix to assist you in documenting a plan. Just remember, aim to first reduce the debt that has the highest interest rate.

Chapter O Learn a new <u>standard money operation</u>. How do you manage your money? Do you save some or do you spend it all? Well, it doesn't matter if you have a massive amount, small amount or no amount; your standard operation will be the same. Your standard operation is based on your internal upbringing and environmental teachings. This chapter will teach you a new technique. Consider following this cash flow operation: you get cash, pay bills and set aside funds for personal goals with the practice to having leftovers for saving. It's just that simple. Read this chapter for the detailed instructions.

Chapter P Peas in the Pot - pray, plan, pay and play. This is truly the Pea-Chapter or the Penny-Chapter. This is the time when you sit with the family to discuss how you expect to take each paycheck and spread it out until the next pay period. With each check you should follow these steps: pray over it, plan for it, pay bills with it and play around it. The whole family should take a personal interest in setting up the budget. Once the budget is complete, your path is to carry it wherever you go. I recommend that the family make a total commitment by promising to use the budget as a major tool to managing the funds. <u>Work the budget with patience while prioritizing the</u>

many, many expenses. Each family member has the power to endure such a task. The point to remember is not to spend more than the pennies that you have available to you. So take pleasure in operating the budget, but do so promptly and effectively.

Chapter Q

It is time for a quiz. You must take this test in order to spend money. This chapter shows you how to implement a budget and how to incorporate a picture ID for spending purposes. There are 10 steps to this quiz; conduct each one step at a time. Once this test is complete, the next time you work through this process will be six months. At the end of this assignment, sit back and smile as you have succeeded by accomplishing a great task: the family's budget. If by chance you have some leftovers, then you are indeed on your way to completing the alphabet with high scores.

Chapter R

Release the old; build a (new) road map. This chapter avails you to draw up a new map in order for the family to get to the place called success. You will need the following tools to endure the journey. You will need a **GPS - Gas up** with a **P**urposeful **S**avings plan. The GPS is required to ensure that the family does not run out of gas before getting to its destination. Also, you will need gears called save: **S**=sacrifice; **A**=advance; **V**=visualize and victory; **E**=excel or excellence. The save gears are required to ensure that the family is equipped for the long haul. It doesn't have to be an unpleasant trip as long as you are prepared and you planned ahead for the mission. Read the chapter for the other tools needed for the trip down 'success' avenue.

Chapter S

Save, save, and save even if the interest rates are low. There are six reasons why you should save; they are provided by tiers. In addition to saving at each tier, you must develop a savings plan as well as a savings policy. The plan details where the money is coming from, how much, how often and the expected timeframe goal. The policy documents what the funds will be used for. This savings regimen will be shared with the members of the family with the intention for them to follow the agreed upon savings objectives.

Chapter T

Stop focusing on Taxes! Taxes existed from the beginning of time and there will not be a time whereas taxation will cease to exist. Remove your focus from paying taxes and <u>focus on making money</u>. Look at the big picture: increasing your portfolio. This may include paying more taxes, but do not fret over that. Just take advantage of those deductions, credits and exemptions. If you qualify for them, by all means take them. This chapter stresses that you should not live by the complicated tax code law alone. You should enjoy your life, make decisions that are best suited for the family and pay your taxes. Tax codes will change but paying taxes are here to stay.

Chapter U

Are you uninsured or underinsured? Both options are unfavorable. Not having insurance or not having sufficient insurance is risky. This chapter will explain why you need insurance. But, most importantly, the family unit must decide the level of risks its willing to partake. The question to ask yourself is whether you need a **<u>large umbrella</u>** or a small one. There will be unexpected events to occur in your life, but it is up to you to decide whether you need that extra **<u>peace of mind</u>** by obtaining the adequate amounts of insurance.

Chapter V & W

You are almost there. You are now ready to climb that pyramid from victory to financial independence to becoming the grand winner. You are not just looking to be wealthy but to fulfill your purpose in life. You have goals to be documented, objectives to meet, dreams to accomplish and a mission to complete. Yes, all of these things take money, but you are ready for the tasks at hand. You know how to obtain that wealth. Now you are focused on the prize.

Chapter X Eliminate the negatives in your life. Get rid of those negative people, places, things and ideas. Also, eliminate those negative words. Never react from negative statements or thoughts. Release the negative and replace with positive phrases. Let's start with the following statement. Can you become wealthy – yes, you can. In conclusion, take notes on the correlation between negativity and financial dependence. Now, eliminate the thought, X out any negatives. Quit the negatives and **hire the positives**. You now have direction, work towards the positive plans that will have a direct and meaningful impact financially on each family member.

Chapter Y & Z This chapter presents a proclamation for immediate release. Recite this statement as this will be your year-round plan that must be followed with zeal. Open the family meetings with this statement and close with a prayer. With God's help and by remembering the financial alphabet written in this book, the family will be able to continue striving for the good of the household. Repeat the chapters as needed and press forward to obtaining and maintaining first-class rate financial managerial skills.

Afterword – My Personal ABCs

My **attitude has changed** since my long standing of unemployment and my struggle to regain a full-time job. Ever since my first job at Landmark Bank, I thought the amount in one's bank account decided the status of that person. How I felt about myself was based on how much money I had in all of my accounts. My outlook on life was dependent upon the size of my accounts and that size affected my daily routine which was based on my current financial situation. This assumption is probably how many people feel. Even though, money can get you to places that you have never been before, dreaming can also get you to those same places. You need to have direction in your life and not get stuck when you get to a road block. There are more ways than one to get where you want to be. Most people thought that unemployment would be the show stopper. It was not and it will never be. Previously, my confidence level was based on my job and how much I was getting paid. Well, I have been unemployed for over than two years and I have no money in my account. As a matter of fact, I had to close down several of my accounts, because they had dwindled down to zero and the banks were beginning to charge me a monthly fee. It is amazing how my circumstances have changed me – but God is always constant in my life. I wake up every morning knowing that I have no job and no money, yet I feel great about myself. Of course, there is a great deal of things that cost money, but there are a bunch of things that are free. I know this because I have found them. You just have to search for them. When I drop off my child to school, I go to work. I do not go to a place of employment that pays me for my time. I go to the library to search for training classes, local conferences, workshops that are free. I go to the library to check out books to stay current on my profession. This is how I work while I am unemployed. My **behavior has changed;** I do not spend my limited funds on frivolous stuff. I pay close attention to everything I spend. There are times I spend too much effort on the small stuff. This is something I continue to strive to become better in this area. My **character has changed** significantly. I am more giving. I give more of myself as well as I give a large percentage of my unemployment pay. There have been a huge number of people who have given to me during this time;

therefore, I must give back to those in need of my assistance. My **ABCs level-headedness** is because I continue to remain positive.

I am a penny pincher. I guess I will always be. I think I have gotten worst. My nick name is **"CENT"** and I think this is because I can take a penny and stretch it until I am able to obtain another one. Nevertheless, those copper coins do add up and they have multiplied over the years. This is how I have been living for the past two years. Now, my daughter picks up pennies. I have not taught her this action. Yet, I have accepted that this is a great habit to have – she is climbing her own financial ladder one penny at a time. My 10-year-old daughter has sense by not throwing away her cent$.

I never tried to get away with the four Bs: buying, begging, biting and borrowing. However, I have attempted to be a part of any assistance program that was open and available for my family. One day, I stood out in 99 degree weather for approximately three hours to get a pair of shoes for my daughter. We nearly passed out, still we ended up with no shoes; it was too hot to wait out the long process. Though, I never begged I still wanted to be on the front-line for any type assistance while I was unemployed. **I was not ashamed to request monetary assistance**, but it took me a long time to get to this point. It didn't matter if the organization wanted to pay my creditors directly. I went through the application process and I tried to wait patiently.

Speaking of those creditors, I recognized early in the game that they are people too. Really, they are individuals just like you and me. I always made an effort to treat them nice and say a kind word. Some have the ability to waive your credit charges. When I noticed that my customer service representative was in a good mood, I would request that he/she waive my interest charges and late fees. Please note that I did not beg; I suggested this based on my credit history. If I noticed that he/she was not in a good mood, I would end the conversation quickly and say, "Have a great day." Subsequently, I would call back in hopes to get someone else on the line that was having a better day. On the other hand, it was a fact that some of my creditors were left trying to squeeze funds out of me that was dried up like plums with no incoming flow (I mean source) from anything steady. All my reliable funds were down the toilet and were being flushed out by my biggest debt, my mortgage, health costs and by the hot summer, which was reflected in my utility bill. All the same, it was up to me to decide who to pay first and **I was never pressured to pay anyone from those harassing calls and letters.** All of the folks that threatened to send me to the collection agency did not scare me – only two followed through. But when I signed a contract or made an agreement to pay a bill, **I kept my word.** I never placed a STOP payment on a check that I agreed to pay. I am surviving because of my good word and not due to the size of my pocketbook. Right now, I have no money but I am trusted to pay up eventually.

In the meanwhile, I have obtained grant money from the governmental stimulus program and monetary blessings from nonprofit organizations such as my church. As for non-monetary assistance, I would go around eating free meals whenever I could. I am not embarrassed by that. I love to eat and I needed to eat. I would participate in free Church meals, open house events, friends treating me, lunch specials for the unemployed and sometimes volunteered to get a free meal. I could not afford even the basic essentials and most times I skipped breakfast, so that "pride" thing did not have any effect on me grabbing a free bite to eat. I would get a personal invitation due to my circumstances and I always accepted. I even packed a plate or two for dinner that night, if I was allowed to do such a thing.

While I was unemployed, *my cash took off and left me first.* I had 6 months' worth of reserve. From my managing, I was able to stretch it out for almost a year. My capital which was my house, maintained its status quo. There were no huge increases or decreases to my capital. I focused on paying off my car note, and it helped my bills some; however, the value of the car decreased. I was still happy because the car was drivable. My good name and credit rating stayed the longest at the highest range possible. Therefore, I was able to borrow funds, if necessary, to cover the living expenses not met by any other means. I did not have to borrow funds – maybe just a small line-of-credit. I stayed within four figures of my unsecured credit line. Thank goodness that while I had a job, I set aside funds for a rainy day. Well, it has been raining for over 700 days, **but I am covered by the grace of God.**

My life for the past two years has been overwhelmingly full of challenges, short falls, spiritual growth and blessings. There was a time when I owed an individual business owner where I overpaid for her services by $5.00. I mentioned to her that it was my gift; and I ordered her to keep it. I wanted to give as others have given to me. A month later, I asked for it back because I thought I needed it to pay a more urgent bill. At the time, I thought I would be short. Well, needless to say that I fell one to two steps backwards on my own financial ladder to success. Somehow, I lost faith (temporarily). It appears that sometimes I forget how far God has brought me. Therefore, I have started keeping a journal to jot down my journey. I review it every so often to witness to others and myself on how far I have come. I wrote this over a year ago:

> *I am thankful for what comes my way, but sometimes I feel that I am **drowning**. Nevertheless, I am still floating because I do volunteer work and I have a great support system: my sister Gwendolyn, my church family & friends, my neighbor, my sorority and my 83 year old mentor. Also, I preach to others on why they should **not** use their credit cards unnecessarily, but I have and I do on a regular basis. I want to write a book on my experience and on how to survive during the difficult times, but sometimes I have these hunger pains. My current struggles and pains are keeping me from writing freely. So for now, those diminutives yet necessary items I buy, may cost $750 today, but with added credit card interest charges the costs will likely rise to over $1,000 next quarter. The fact is, I do not even have a **quarter** and I need a stash until I obtain that job with some income again. As a single parent, I just want to feel secure and safe again for the well-being of my family.*

Well, I am here to say that I have not drowned and I am paying down on my credit card. Above all, I have written this book while going through my biggest financial struggle yet. Through God who has strengthened me, I said to my hands, "fingers do not fail me now." At first, I was standing still, all the while praying. Now, I am **back** climbing my financial ladder through my winning dreams and upward hope. *I have made good from my unemployment – I have written a book. I made good, because God is my Author.*

Bibliography

The following books are recommended as an additional resource of personal financial management. If you need more in depth knowledge, the library and the Web provide numerous excellent materials for a wider range and comprehensive coverage on the subject matter at hand. If managing your personal finances is new for you, then these books along will *add value* to what has already been provided in this book.

Ernst & Young LLP. (1996). *Personal Financial Planning Guide.* New York: John Wiley & Sons, Inc.

Garman/Forgue. (2008). *Personal Finance.* Boston, MA: Houghton Mifflin Company.

Kiyosaki, R. T. (2008). *Increase Your Financial IQ.* New York: Business Plus: Hachette Book Group.

Lawrence, J. (2008). *The Budget Kit.* New York: Kaplan Publishing.

Openshaw, J. (2004). *Quick & Easy Budget Kit.* Family Financial Network's.

Ramsey, D. (2003). *The Total Money Makeover.* Nashville, TN: Thomas Nelson, Inc.

Stephens, B. (1997). *Talking Dollars and Making Sense.* New York: McGraw-Hill.

Appendix –
sixteen steps to climbing the ladder

To successfully climb your financial ladder to wealth, take the time out to journey through the 16 steps of this appendix included for referential, educational, entertainment, planning and/or motivational purposes.

Step 1	Two (Financial) Our Daily Bread
Step 2	Your Pledge to Stop
Step 3	My Personal Financial Contracts
Step 4	My Personal Payoff Contract
Step 5	A Piece of the Pie
Step 6	Minor Purchase Pass
Step 7	Permission Slip to Spend
Step 8	Spending ID Card with instructions
Step 9	Balance Sheet
Step 10	Home Contents Inventory List
Step 11	Debt Schedule
Step 12	Detailed Income Items (Budget Part A)
Step 13	Expense Items (Budget Part B)
Step 14	Working Capital and Net-Worth
Step 15	Statement of Cash Flows
Step 16	Cash Calendar

Two (Financial) Our Daily Bread

Widow's Gift of Two Mites

Mark 12:41-44

Jesus sat in the temple near the treasury and watched as people walked by and deposited their gifts for the temple. Some made a show of it, perhaps so others could see how much they had given. Just then a poor woman came by and threw in two "mites".

A mite was the least valuable coin in circulation. Thus the widow's gift was very small, amounting to nothing in most folk's eyes. But our Lord saw what others did not see. She had given "all that she had". The widow wasn't trying to draw attention to herself. She was simply doing what she was ABLE to do. And Jesus noticed.

God looks at the heart, not the hand; the giver, not the gift.

Our Daily Bread
RBC Ministries
Grand Rapids, MI

True Wealth

1 Timothy 6:17-18

Money is a powerful force. We work for it, save it, spend it, use it to satisfy our earthside longings, and then wish we had more. Aware of its distracting danger, Jesus taught more about money than any other topic. And, as far as we know, He never took an offering for Himself. Clearly, He didn't teach about giving to fill His own pockets. Instead, Jesus warned us that trusting in wealth and using it to gain power clogs our spiritual arteries more readily than most other impediments to spiritual development. In telling the story of the "rich fool," He shamed His listeners for not being rich toward God (Luke 12:13-21), indicating that God has a far different definition of wealth than most of us.

So, what does it mean to be rich toward God? Paul tells us that those who are rich should not be conceited about their wealth, "nor to trust in uncertain riches." Rather, we are to "be rich in good works, ready to give, willing to share."

Interesting! God measures wealth by the quality of our lives and our generous use of wealth to bless others. Not exactly Wall Street insider talk, but great advice for those of us who think that our security and reputation are tied up in the size of our bank account.

If we've been blessed with riches,
We must be rich in deeds;
God wants us to be generous
In meeting others' needs.

Riches are a blessing only to those who make them a blessing to others.

Written by: Our Daily Bread

Your Pledge to Stop

STOP trying to keep up with the Joneses. Respect their goods and get your own free and clear.

STOP trying so hard to make a million bucks when you have no dreams or goals written down. Develop your own purpose and direction in life and go after the dreams not the BUCKS!

STOP complaining about things that you do not have and you are not willing to work hard to obtain.

STOP saying that you are bored with your life. Do something with your life by using your God given gifts to become financial independent.

STOP blaming your ancestors for your financial problems. Talk about solutions with your immediate family and then implement them.

STOP buying things when you know that you cannot afford them. If you cannot control your impulse spending, then quit going to the stores.

STOP using credit to buy things, especially when you don't NEED the items anyway.

STOP spending foolishly and eating your money away. Allow a budget to be your leading guide.

STOP maintaining worthless assets. Dispose of all assets and liabilities that bring your financial net-worth down.

STOP letting family members and friends tie up your cash. Tell them to manage their own cash flow troubles.

STOP packing your house, storage and walk-in-closets with "stuff". Focus on your long-term goals and pursue those purchases with caution.

STOP failing to pay your bills; follow through with all of your financial commitments. Be true to your word.

STOP lying to yourself that you do not need to budget and save. It is not okay to walk out of the house without your personalized budget and savings plan.

STOP pulling people along the path to your final destination when it is obvious they do not believe in you or your goals. Either they want to be a part of your dreams or they need to jump ship immediately.

STOP listening to negative people! Do not allow that virus to spread into your household.

STOP taking in sad and depressing activity, especially if the activity leaves you with little or no hope. Take the risk on pursuing your own passions.

STOP making excuses about where you are in life and why you cannot do what you want to do. Look around, the world does not stop turning for you or your excuses.

STOP allowing FEAR to hold you back. Face your fears head on by taking advantage of the tools provided in this book.

STOP performing the same old thing that is not working in your life. Motivate yourself and make a change. Try something different. Look to this book for new techniques.

STOP waiting on others to tell you when to move and how to move forward. Start by setting your own direction, obtain assistance from those willing to encourage you to step up to the plate and then work out a plan!

STOP quitting and giving up too soon before accomplishing those dreams. Take precautions on managing your finances along with enforcing the experiences that you want. Paste yourself and personally fulfill those commitments. Complete your God given assignments with a sufficient level of gas for the journey by Praying, Planning, Paying and Playing.

What are you going to **stop** doing today?
There are 21 **STOP** statements.
Recite one statement daily until you have completed them all!
Do this for 21 days and note a change in your life.

My Personal Financial Contracts

ON________________, I____
BEING OF SOUND MIND, HAVE THE FOLLOWING DREAMS THAT WILL BE ACCOMPLISHED BEFORE MY TIME (ON EARTH) IS COMPLETE.

MY PERSONAL DREAMS:	FIRST STEP	STARTING DATE
________________________	__________	______________
________________________	__________	______________
________________________	__________	______________
________________________	__________	______________
________________________	__________	______________
________________________	__________	______________

THE FUNDS WILL BE PLACED IN A(N) __________________ ACCOUNT AND I HAVE AGREED NOT TO WITHDRAW ANY MONEY FROM THIS ACCOUNT UNLESS IT IS AN EMERGENCY.

BY________________, 20_____, I PLAN TO OBTAIN $_________

SIGNED BY: ___________________

WITNESSED BY: ________________

My Personal Financial Contracts

ON_______________, I_________________________________
BEING OF SOUND MIND, HAVE ESTABLISHED THE FOLLOWING

LONG TERM GOALS:	PRESENT VALUE	FUTURE VALUE
____________________	________________	_______________
____________________	________________	_______________
____________________	________________	_______________
____________________	________________	_______________
____________________	________________	_______________
____________________	________________	_______________

THE FUNDS WILL BE PLACED IN A(N) ___________________ ACCOUNT AND I HAVE AGREED NOT TO WITHDRAW ANY MONEY FROM THIS ACCOUNT UNLESS IT IS AN EMERGENCY.

BY________________, 20_____, I PLAN TO OBTAIN $_________

SIGNED BY: ___________________

WITNESSED BY: ________________

My Personal Payoff Contract

ON________________, I_______________________________________
BEING OF SOUND MIND, HAVE ESTABLISHED THE FOLLOWING PAYOFF GOALS:

CREDITOR'S NAME	$DOLLAR AMOUNT	PAYOFF DATE
____________________	________________	_______________
____________________	________________	_______________
____________________	________________	_______________
____________________	________________	_______________
____________________	________________	_______________
____________________	________________	_______________

THE OUTSTANDING DEBT(S) WILL BE PAID ON-TIME MONTHLY AND I HAVE AGREED NOT TO STOP THE PAYMENTS UNTIL PAID-IN-FULL. ALSO, I HAVE AGREED NOT TO MAKE ANY MAJOR PURCHASES UNLESS IT IS A NECESSITY AND AN EMERGENCY.

BY_________________, 20_____, I WILL TREAT MYSELF TO SOMETHING NOT TO EXCEED $__________.

SIGNED BY: ___________________

WITNESSED BY: ________________

A Piece of the Pie

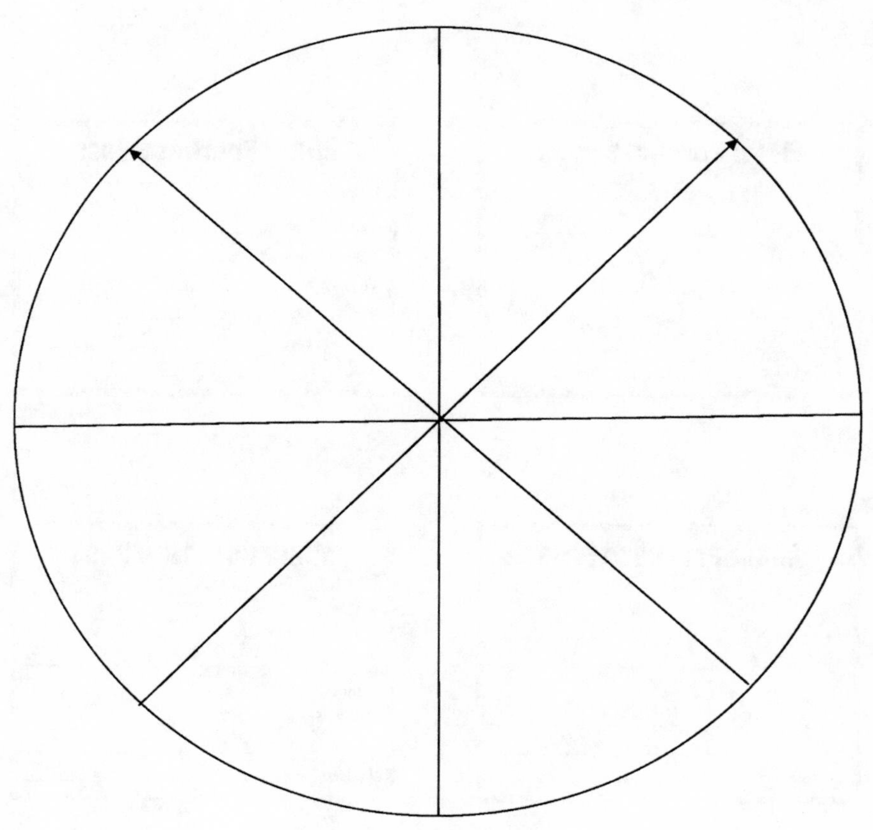

Minor Purchase Pass

Family Member: ______________________

Date Needed: ______________________

Store Name: ______________________

Max to Spend: ______________________

Actual Spent: ______________________

Budget Line: ______________________

Minor Purchase Pass

Family Member: ______________________

Date Needed: ______________________

Store Name: ______________________

Max to Spend: ______________________

Actual Spent: ______________________

Budget Line: ______________________

Minor Purchase Pass

Family Member: ______________________

Date Needed: ______________________

Store Name: ______________________

Max to Spend: ______________________

Actual Spent: ______________________

Budget Line: ______________________

Minor Purchase Pass

Family Member: ______________________

Date Needed: ______________________

Store Name: ______________________

Max to Spend: ______________________

Actual Spent: ______________________

Budget Line: ______________________

Minor Purchase Pass

Family Member: ______________________

Date Needed: ______________________

Store Name: ______________________

Max to Spend: ______________________

Actual Spent: ______________________

Budget Line: ______________________

Minor Purchase Pass

Family Member: ______________________

Date Needed: ______________________

Store Name: ______________________

Max to Spend: ______________________

Actual Spent: ______________________

Budget Line: ______________________

Permission Slip to Spend!

Trip to store details			**What to bring**
Store Name	____________	☑	Food treats to eat so that you will not have an empty stomach and have some tolerance to compare and negotiate what you need. **Note**: This is particularly necessary when grocery shopping.
Date	____________	☑	Spending license and shopping list.
Time	30 minutes to 1 hour max.	☑	Hand-held calculator (to compute discounts, savings, etc.)
Budget Category	____________	☑	Budget Partner. **(Optional)**
Budget Amount	$__________ to cover ____________	⊘	**Note**: Do not go to the store when you have nothing else to do. Be strict with your time limitation in the store. Do not go to the store when you are depressed or unhappy about something. Try not to go to the store with young children especially if you are gullible.
Explanation and Notes	____________ ____________ ____________ ____________		

✂- -

Cut off bottom portion of permission slip and return to a family member at least 24 hours before the shopping day.

In case of emergency, please contact:

______________________________ ______________

Name/Relationship **Phone**

Special Instructions: (Who to call if attempted to overspend in store…must call before you get to check-out line)

I give permission to (family name),__________________a trip to the store (name of store) ______________________________. This permission will expire on _______/_______/________.

Enclosed is extra $__________ to cover the cost of the purchase(s). Amount must be within the budget.

Method of payment: _____cash _____ check _____debit card _____credit card (Name of card: ____________)

X ______________________________ ______________

Head or Co-Head of Household **Date**

Spending ID Card with Instructions

The instructions are available to show you how to set your identification number. Please fill in the blanks completely as this will provide the classification for your spending ID card with a calculated allowance. Follow these instructions after the family's budget is set as this will be the ID card that should be carried with you at all times.

Column 1: Family household number:

The first digit represents the number in your family within the household. You are only allowed one digit. If your family is greater than nine (9), then you will need to review the members that are 18 years old and greater. The family members may live in the same household but have their own income. If this is the case, then they should have a separate budget. You would only count the husband, wife and other non-income making dependents in slot one.

Column 2: Years until retirement:

The second and third digits represent the number of years before retirement. You would subtract the year you plan to retire from the current year. If you plan to retire in < 10 years, then you would place a zero as the first digit and the actual number as the second digit. If you plan to retire in 10 years or greater, then you would use the actual number in this two digit slot.

Column 3: Emergency Fund (3-6 months):

Do you have at least 3 months worth of "emergency funds"? If the answer is "NO", then place **NO** in the third slot for your ID number.

Answer the following questions to know how many months are needed in case of an emergency.

Base number of emergency funds needed is 3 months; write three (3) on this line: ____________.

Are you in a single parent household or a two-adult household with one income? If yes, write one (1) on this line: ____________.

Are there dependents 4 years old or younger in the household? If yes, write one (1) on this line:

____________.

Do you have a household of at least 5 members? If yes, write one (1) on this line: ____________.

Add up the numbers noted from the questions above: ____________. If you have at least this number X (times) your monthly gross income set aside for any emergency, place YES in the 3rd slot. If not, place NO in there. Set a goal to work towards saving enough for an emergency that will most likely occur in your life.

Column 4: The Allowance:

Once you have completed the budget, you will be able to compute your allowance amount. You can set up a weekly, bimonthly or monthly allowance. I would not recommend setting up an allowance that is longer than one month or shorter than one week. Usually, an allowance will be around $100 per period per family member. This amount represents a personal spending amount that would not be tracked for budgeting purposes. This is your free money to spend at your free will over the base-line budget.

Column 5: Place an "X" in the 5th slot; this is consistent on all ID's.

Column 6: The Multiplier:

For a weekly allowance, use 52 for self-payment of once a week.
For a biweekly allowance, use 26 for self-payment of every other wk.

For a bimonthly allowance, use 24 for self-payment of twice a month.
For a monthly allowance, use 12 for self-payment of once a month.

Column 7: Restrictions:

Debit Card – Do you keep a daily record of all charges that hit your account? Do you stay within your daily account balance? Do you spend only what's in your budget? If you answered, "yes" to all of the questions then you are able to maintain use of the debit card with no restrictions. If you answer "no" to any one of these questions, then you will have restrictions.

Credit Card – Do you have an outstanding balance less than 1% of your income? Do you spend only what's within your budget? If you answered, "yes" to both questions then you are able to maintain use of the credit card with no restrictions. If you have an outstanding balance between 1% and 10% of your income then you will have SOME restrictions. If you have an outstanding balance greater than 10% of your income, then you will note CREDIT CARD under restrictions on the "Spend Card".

Less than 1% debt	No credit card restrictions
Between 1% and 10%	Some restrictions (see notes below)
Greater than 10%	Credit Card restricted

Here are the points that must be followed for the term "SOME" restrictions:

- Currently able to use the credit card as long as purchased items are within the budget.
- Must make credit card payments greater than the minimum amount required.
- Extra cash received must go towards paying off credit card(s)' outstanding balance.
- Stop using card, if balance goes above the 10% balance.

Here are your personalized grade and class levels. These are your spending ID class levels. These classifications are temporary. You are allowed to update your status every 6 months. See **Chapter Q** for a more detailed description.

- **Class A** – You have Full **A**uthorization. This is the highest level.

- **Class B** – You have a Minor Im**b**alance in your budget.

- **Class C** – You are low on **C**ash. Your cash allowance should reflect this.

- **Class D** – You have a major **D**eficit in your budget.

- **Class E** – You are only able to spend so that you can physically **e**at.

- **Class F** – You **F**ailed the test. The family must sit down together and retake the quiz.

The Spending ID Card

My Spending License
Class: A **Expires: June or Dec.**
Restrictions: No Debit Card
Daily Maximum Spend Amount: $30/week
Budget: ON FILE
In case of emergency call:
My Neighbor - Carolyn

Cynthia Elliott

ID #215YES30X52

Signature

Here are the CLASS types:

A - Full authorization.
B - Minor imbalance?
C - Low on CASH.
D - Major deficit.
E - Only spend enough to EAT!
F - Frankly you have FAILED the test!!

The Spending ID Card

Insert picture from file HERE

My Spending License
Class: **Expires: June or Dec.**
Restrictions: No???
Daily Maximum Spend Amount:
Budget: ON FILE
In case of emergency call:
Best Friend -

Your Name

ID ###NO##X##

Signature

Here are the CLASS types:

A - Full authorization.
B - Minor imbalance?
C - Low on CASH.
D - Major deficit.
E - Only spend enough to EAT!
F - Frankly you have FAILED the test!!

Insert your own picture, name, ID# and spending license stipulations.

ID#: The first number in the ID represents the number in your household.
Only one digit should be used.
The second & third spaces represent the number of years before retirement.
NO - represents that you do not have an emergency fund.
YES - represents that you do have some type of emergency fund.
The next slot represents your allowance amount.
X - means times. Consistent on all ID's.
The final slot represents your allowance period. Do not use a daily allowance.
For example, use 52 if you have a weekly allowance.
Use 26 if you have a biweekly allowance.
Use 24 if you have a bimonthly allowance.
Use 12 if you have a monthly allowance.

Balance Sheet

ASSETS

Current Assets

Cash on hand	
Cash in bank	
Savings/CD's	
Inventory	
Short-term investments (stocks, bonds)	
Other	
Total Current Assets	

Fixed Assets

Business investments	
Personal investments (antiques, etc.)	
Land only	
My principal house	
My investment house	
My vehicles	
Computer & Electronic Equipment	
Furniture and fixtures	
Total Net Fixed Assets	

TOTAL ASSETS	

RATIOS

Current Ratio	
Quick Ratio	
Cash Ratio	

LIABILITIES

Current Liabilities

Basic bills	
Short-term notes	
Current portion of long-term notes	
Taxes payable	
Student loan debt	
Credit card debt	
Total Current Liabilities	

Long-term Liabilities

Mortgage	
Other long-term liabilities	
Total Long-Term Liabilities	

Total Liabilities	

NET WORTH

Net Worth	
The __________Family's Net Worth	

TOTAL LIAB. & NET WORTH	

Home Contents Inventory List

Home Contents Inventory List

Name	
Address	
Phone	
Insurance policy number	
Insurance agent	
Insurance agent phone	
Insurance company	
Insurance company phone	
Total estimated value (add values from each page)	

Tip: *It's a good idea to save a paper copy of this list in a fireproof safe, safe deposit box, or somewhere outside of your home.*

Room/area	Item/description	Make/model	Serial number/ ID number	Date purchased	Where purchased	Purchase price	Estimated current value	Notes (photo?)	Code (X, Y, Z, XY, XZ, XYZ)

Home Contents Inventory List

Room/area	Item/description	Make/model	Serial number/ ID number	Date purchased	Where purchased	Purchase price	Estimated current value	Notes (photo?)	Code (X, Y, Z, XY, XZ, XYZ)

Debt Schedule

A Practice Sheet

As of December 31, 2010

Creditor's Name	Original Amt Borrowed	Maturity Date	Interest Rate	Promise To Pay	Ending Bal
Sears	$ 1,500		8.96%	$ 66	$ 993
Discover Card	$ 1,600		11.87%	$ 60	$ 1,333
First TN LOC	$ 2,000	revolving	12.00%	$200	$ 2,000
Best Buy	$ 2,500		12.50%	$ 25	$ 2,250
Student Loan	$ 600		6.00%	$100	$ 600
Furniture Store	$ 9,894	refinanced	6.99%	$250	$ 9,700
Grand Total	$18,094			$701	$16,876

*** How much do you promise to pay each month until the ending balance is ZERO?

Which creditor, are you going to pay off first? Focus on the high-interest rate debt first.

Complete the "Personal Payoff Contract" provided in the Appendix.

Debt Schedule

The Real Thing

As of December 31, 2011

Creditor's Name	Original Amt Borrowed	Maturity Date	Interest Rate	Promise To Pay	Ending Bal
Grand Total					

Detailed Income Items (Budget Part A)

DETAILED INCOME ITEMS				
	HOW MUCH?	HOW OFTEN?	MONTHLY AMOUNT	GUARANTEED?
SOURCE				yes or no
Head's First Job				
Head's Second Job				
Co-Head's First Job				
Co-Head's Second Job				
Side Business Income				
Interest Income				
Dividend Income				
Royalty Income				
Rental Income				
Trust Fund				
Alimony				
Child Support				
AFDC - Gov't Assistance				
Unemployment				
Social Security				
Pension				
Annuity				
Disability Income				
Cash Gifts				
Other				
TOTAL				

Note: Do not count on the non-guaranteed amounts. Do not include the "no" responses in the budget.

Expense Items (Budget Part B)

EXPENSE ITEMS	HOW MUCH?	HOW OFTEN?	MONTHLY AMOUNT	Code X-delete; Y-reduce; Z-necessity
CHARITABLE GIFTS				
Church/Holy Temple				
Non-profit Organizations				
SAVINGS				
Emergency Fund				
College Fund				
Retirement Fund				
HOUSING				
First Mortgage				
Second Mortgage				
Property Taxes				
Homeowner's (or Renter's) Insurance				
Home Improvement Projects				
Home Furnishings and/or Decorating				
Repairs or Maintenance Fees				
Computer/Electronics Service Plans				
Hardware/Software Upgrades				
Storage Fee				
Yard Work/Garden Supplies				
Pest/Termite Control				
Security System				
Association Dues				
Other				
TOTAL - page 1				

EXPENSE ITEMS	HOW MUCH?	HOW OFTEN?	MONTHLY AMOUNT	Code X-delete; Y-reduce; Z-necessity
UTILITIES				
Electricity				
Gas				
Water				
Home Base - Phone				
Cell Phone				
Trash and Waste Management				
Internet Service Provider/Cable				
FOOD				
Grocery list shopping				
Convenient shopping - (no list)				
Formal Dining out				
Fast Food				
Warehouse Clubs Membership				
TRANSPORTATION				
Vehicle #1 Payment				
Vehicle #2 Payment				
Car Insurance				
Auto Club (such as, AAA)				
Repairs and Tires				
Gas and Oil				
License and Taxes				
Vehicle Inspection				
Transit, Tolls and Parking Fees				
TOTAL - page 2				

EXPENSE ITEMS	HOW MUCH?	HOW OFTEN?	MONTHLY AMOUNT	Code X-delete; Y-reduce; Z-necessity
CHILDREN AND PETS				
Child Support				
Tuition/College Expenses				
School Lunches				
School (K-12) Supplies				
Personal Items				
Summer Camp Fees/Supplies				
Sports Equipment and Toys				
Private Lessons/Recitals/Costumes				
Clothing & Shoes				
Dry Cleaning/Alterations/Shoe Repair				
Child Care and/or Baby Sitter				
Infant Expenses (such as diapers, etc.)				
Pet Food				
Grooming/Pet Hotel				
Vet Expense/Shots/Dental/Other				
Pet Training/License/Tags				
MEDICAL/HEALTH				
Disability Insurance & Long-term Care				
Health Insurance				
Life Insurance				
Doctor Visits (co-payments)				
Dental Exams				
Vision Exams				
Therapy Expense				
Other Health Exams/Visits				
Medications/Prescriptions				
TOTAL - page 3				

EXPENSE ITEMS	HOW MUCH?	HOW OFTEN?	MONTHLY AMOUNT	Code X-delete; Y-reduce; Z-necessity
PERSONAL/RECREATION				
Spousal Support - Alimony				
Work Clothes/Uniforms/Shoes				
Personal Type Clothing				
Dry Cleaning/Alterations/Shoe Repair				
Toiletries				
Cosmetics				
Hair Care				
Education/Adult				
School Tuition				
School Books and Supplies				
Leisure Courses/Classes				
Subscriptions				
Professional Organizational Dues				
Professional Service Fees				
Health Fitness Club Dues				
Sports Equipment				
Gifts, Cards, Flowers				
Entertainment (Movies, Concerts, etc.)				
Vacation				
Miscellaneous 1				
Miscellaneous 2				
Miscellaneous 3				
TOTAL - page 4				

EXPENSE ITEMS	HOW MUCH?	HOW OFTEN?	MONTHLY AMOUNT	Code X-delete; Y-reduce; Z-necessity
DEBTS				
Unsecured Credit				
Secured Loans				
Student Loans				
Extra Credit Line				
IRS Taxes Due				
Other				
Other				
Other				
TOTAL - page 1				
TOTAL - page 2				
TOTAL - page 3				
TOTAL - page 4				
TOTAL - page 5				
TOTAL EXPENSES - PAGE 1-5				
TOTAL HOUSEHOLD INCOME				
DIFFERENCE SHOULD BE POSITIVE				

Working Capital/Net Worth

Calculation Worksheet
Supplementary Information
For the current period ending

WORKING CAPITAL

CURRENT ASSETS

add up all current assets for the family

minus

CURRENT LIABILITIES

add up all current liabilities (debt) for the family

equals

WORKING CAPITAL

the difference between the current assets and current liabilities
the difference is what you have to work with; current funds available

NET WORTH

TOTAL ASSETS

add up all of your assets for the family

minus

TOTAL LIABILITIES

add up all of your liabilities (debt) for the family

equals

NET WORTH

the difference between total assets and total liabilities
the difference is what you are worth

*** see detailed definition of terms in the Glossary ***

Working Capital/Net Worth

List of Items

For the current period ending

Listed items	Type	Asset
Cash on hand	Short Term	✓
Savings account	Short Term	✓
CD account	Short Term	✓
Money-Market Funds	Short Term	✓
Stocks/Bonds Investment Account	Short Term	✓
Real Estate	Long Term	✓
Vehicle(s)	Long Term	✓
Retirement Accounts	Long Term	✓
Cash Value (Insurance)	Long Term	✓
Household Inventory	Long Term	✓
Personal business equipment	Long Term	✓
Jewelry	Long Term	✓
Antiques	Long Term	✓

Working Capital and Net-Worth

List of Items
For the current period ending

Listed items	Type	Liability
Credit Card Debt 1	Short Term	✓
Credit Card Debt 2	Short Term	✓
Credit Card Debt 3	Short Term	✓
Unsecured Debt 1	Short Term	✓
Unsecured Debt 2	Short Term	✓
Secured Loan ___________	Long Term	✓
Secured Loan ___________	Long Term	✓
IRS Tax Debt	Long Term	✓
Student Loan	Long Term	✓
Child Support Debt	Long Term	✓
Primary Mortgage	Long Term	✓
Secondary Mortgage - equity	Long Term	✓

Statement of Cash Flows

[Time Period]

Cash flows by activity

Cash flows from survival activities	
Cash received from main job, unemployment, retirement fund or social security	
Cash paid for housing and transportation expenses	
Cash paid for food and utilities	
Cash paid for medical/health expenses	
Cash paid for insurance	
Cash paid for payroll taxes	
Other	
Net cash provided (used) for "survival"	

Cash flows from extracurricular activities	
Cash received from alimony, second job, overtime hours and/or tip money	
Cash paid for clothing	
Cash paid for personal/recreational expenses	
Cash paid for pet care expenses	
Cash paid for other non-essentials	
Other	
Net cash provided (used) for "extras"	

Cash flows from dependents' activities	
Cash received from child support (the other parent, family members)	
Cash paid for dependents' clothing	
Cash paid for school expenses	
Cash paid for daycare and/or childcare	
Cash paid for medical/health expenses (children only)	
Cash paid for other essentials	
Other	
Net cash provided (used) for "dependents"	

Statement of Cash Flows

continued - page 2

[Time Period]

Cash flows from investing activities	
Cash received from renter properties, registered businesses and hobbies	
Cash received from personal payroll deduction for investments	
Cash received from investments, such as dividends & interest income	
Cash paid to maintain investment property and business activity	
Cash paid to purchase capital assets, fixed assets, etc.	
Cash paid to savings accounts, CD's and money markets	
Cash paid to retirement accounts, such as IRA, ROTH, 401K	
Other	
Net cash provided (used) for "investing"	

Cash flows from financing activities	
Cash received from personal payroll deduction for garnishments	
Cash received from notes receivables	
Cash received from other borrowings	
Cash paid to charitable organizations	
Cash paid to reduce student loans	
Cash paid to retire short-term or long-term debt	
Cash paid to IRS for past tax debt	
Cash paid to family, friends for a personal loan	
Other	
Net cash provided (used) in "financing"	

Increase (decrease) in cash during the period	
Cash balance at the beginning of the period	
Cash balance at the end of the period	

Cash Calendar

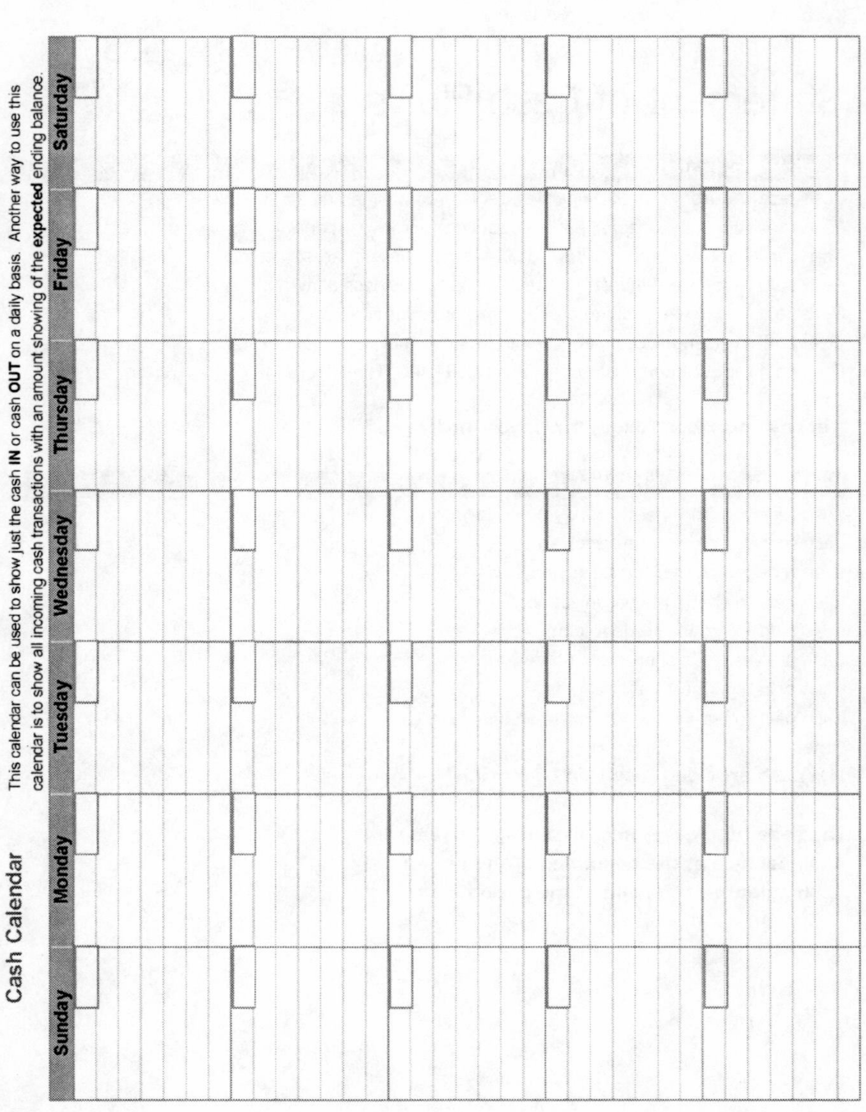
Cash Calendar
This calendar can be used to show just the cash IN or cash OUT on a daily basis. Another way to use this calendar is to show all incoming cash transactions with an amount showing of the expected ending balance.
Sunday
Monday
Tuesday
Wednesday
Thursday
Friday
Saturday

Glossary of Essential Terms

To walk the walk, and talk the talk, learn the terms: The definitions were obtained from www.hyperdictionary.com, **the terms noted with an * were obtained from** www.dictionary.com **and the terms noted with ** are from my professional knowledge as a Certified Public Accountant.**

Allowance - an amount allowed or granted (as during a given period); put on a fixed allowance, as of food.

Aspirations - a cherished desire; a will to succeed.

** **Asset** - a useful or valuable quality. Probable future economic benefits obtained or controlled by the family as a result of past transactions or events. In other words, what do you own? Total assets equal all short-term plus long-term assets.

Attitude - a complex mental state involving beliefs and feelings and values and dispositions to act in certain ways; "he had the attitude that money grew on trees – easily assessible."

Balance Sheet - a record of the financial situation of an institution on a particular date by listing its assets and the claims against those assets.

Behavior - manner of acting or conducting yourself regarding money.

Benefit - something that aids or promotes well-being; "for the common good."

Bill - a statement of money owed for goods or services; "he paid his bill and left"; "send me an account of what I owe"; demand payment; "Will I get charged for this service?"; "We were billed for 4 nights in the hotel, although I stayed only 3 nights."

Borrowing - obtaining funds from a lender, creditor, etc.

Budget - a summary of intended expenditures along with proposals for how to meet them; a sum of money allocated for a particular purpose; "the Adam family runs on a budget of $75,000 a year."

* **Capital** - goods used to generate income either by investing in a business or some other type of income property.

Cash - money in the form of bills or coins; prompt payment for goods or services in currency or by check.

Cash Flow - the excess of cash revenues over cash outlays in a given period of time (not including non-cash expenses).

* **Cash Ratio** - the most conservative liquidity ratio for judging the financial stability of a family on a short-term basis. To calculate cash ratio, add the value of the family's cash and short-term marketable securities and divide the total by current liabilities. This ratio shows the ability of the family's cash on hand to fund short-term liabilities.

Characteristics - typical or distinctive trait...in regards to money management.

Checking Account - a bank account against which the depositor can drawn checks payable on demand.

Checks - a written order directing a bank to pay money; "he paid all his bills by check"; write out a check on a bank account.

Compound Interest - interest calculated on both the principal and the accrued interest.

Compulsive Spending – caused by or suggestive of psychological compulsion to spend.

Contingency Plan - the state of being contingent on a backup plan.

Contributions - act of giving in common with others for a common purpose especially to a charity; a voluntary gift (as of money or service or ideas) made to some worthwhile cause.

Costs - the property of having material worth (often indicated by the amount of money something would bring if sold); "the fluctuating monetary value of gold and silver"; "he puts a high price on his services";

"he couldn't calculate the cost of the collection"; the total spent for goods or services including money and time and labor.

Credit - arrangement for deferred payment for goods and services; have trust in; trust in the truth or veracity of.

Credit Card - a card (usually plastic) that assures a seller that the person using it has a satisfactory credit rating and that the issuer will see to it that the seller receives payment for the merchandise delivered.

** **Current Assets** - Resources that are reasonably expected to be realized in cash, sold, or consumed as a prepaid item during the normal operating cycle of one year or less. These assets are also known as short-term.

** **Current Liabilities** - Obligations that are expected to be required to cover expenditures within the year. In other words, who do you owe and how much do you owe them? In addition, these liabilities are considered short-term debt.

* **Current Ratio** - a measure of a family's ability to meet its short-term obligations. The current ratio is calculated by dividing current assets by current liabilities. Both variables are shown on the balance sheet. A relatively high current ratio compared with those of other families in the same economic class indicates high liquidity and generally conservative management, although it may tend to result in reduced profitability.

Debit - an accounting entry acknowledging sums that are owed.

* **Debit Card** - a plastic card that resembles a credit card but functions like a check and through which payments for purchases or services are made electronically to the bank accounts of participating retailing establishments directly from those of card holders.

Debt - an obligation to pay or do something; money or goods or services owed by one person to another; the state of owing something (especially money); "he is deeply in debt."

Deductible – (for insurance purposes) a clause in an insurance policy that relieves the insurer of responsibility to pay the initial loss up to a stated amount. (for income tax purposes) an amount that can be deducted.

Direct Deposit - electronic deposit of funds into a savings account or checking account. Direct deposit reduces the expense of making payments and the time required to credit payments to an account.

Dividend - that part of the earnings of a corporation that is distributed to its shareholders; usually paid quarterly.

Documentation - confirmation that some fact or statement is true.

Dream - a cherished desire; "his ambition is to own his own business."

Equity - the difference between the market value of a property and the claims held against it; the ownership interest.

Expenditures - the act of consuming something; the act of spending money for goods or services; money paid out.

Expenses - amounts paid for goods and services.

Family - primary social group; parents and children; "he wanted to have a good job before starting a family"; a person having kinship with another or others; "he's kin"; "he's family."

** **Fees** – Money charged to service an account, such as late fees, overdraft fees, over-the-credit limit fees and maintenance fees.

Finance - the commercial activity of providing funds and capital; the management of money and credit and banking and investments; the branch of economics that studies the management of money and other assets; obtain or provide money for; "Can we finance the addition to our home?"; sell or provide on credit.

Fixed - incapable of being changed or moved or undone; e.g. "frozen prices"; "living on fixed income or expenses."

Funds - assets in the form of money.

* **Future Value** - the amount to which a specific sum or series of sums will grow on a given date in the future. The sums are assumed to earn an annual return that is related to the market rate of interest. For example, $1,000 has a future value of $1,120 in one year, assuming an annual return of 12%.

Gift - the act of giving; something acquired without compensation.

Goal - the state of affairs that a plan is intended to achieve and that (when achieved) terminates behavior intended to achieve it; "the ends justify the means."

Impulsive - characterized by undue haste and lack of thought or deliberation; "a hotheaded decision"; "liable to such impulsive acts as hugging strangers"; "an impetuous display of spending and gambling"; "madcap escapades"; determined by chance or impulse or whim rather than by necessity or reason.

Income - the financial gain (earned or unearned) accruing over a given period of time.

Income Tax - a personal tax levied on annual income.

Independence – to not dependent on or conditioned by or relative to anything else; not controlled by a party or interest group.

Insurance - promise of reimbursement in the case of loss; paid to people or companies so concerned about hazards that they have made prepayments to an insurance company; protection against future loss.

Interest - a fixed charge for borrowing money; usually a percentage of the amount borrowed; "how much interest do you pay on your mortgage?"

Inventory - making an itemized list of merchandise or supplies on hand; "the inventory took two days"; a detailed list of all the items in stock; make or include in an itemized record or report; "Inventory all books before the end of the year."

Investment - the act of investing; laying out money or capital in an enterprise with the expectation of profit; money that is invested with an expectation of profit.

Level-headed – described as collected, composed, reasonable, self-possessed, and well-balanced.

** **Liability** - an obligation to pay money to another party; the state of being legally obliged and responsible. Probable future sacrifices of economic benefits arising from present obligations of the family to transfer assets or provide services to creditors in the future as a result of past transactions or events. Basically, you are obtaining debt now so that you are able to benefit from property such as your home today. You live it up now and pay later - the American dream. Total liabilities = the sum of all short-term debt plus (+) all long-term debt.

Line-of-credit - the maximum credit that a customer is allowed.

Liquidity - being in cash or easily convertible to cash.

Loan - the provision of money temporarily (usually at interest); give temporarily; let have for a limited time.

Long-term - relating to or extending over a relatively long time; "a long-term investment."

Map - plan, delineate, or arrange in detail; "map one's future."

Maturity Date - the date on which a financial obligation must be repaid.

Money - the most common medium of exchange; functions as legal tender; "we tried to collect the money he owed us."

* **Net-Worth** - similar to businesses, net-worth (sometimes called net liabilities) is the total assets minus total outside liabilities of an individual or a company. For a company, this is called shareholders' preference and may be referred to as book value. Net-worth is stated as at a particular year in time.

Note - a promise to pay a specified amount on demand or at a certain time; "I had to co-sign his note at the bank."

Objective - the goal intended to be attained (and which is believed to be attainable); "the sole object of her trip was to see her children."

** **Overdraft** – A condition that occurs when an account holder does not have enough money in a checking account to cover transactions from checks, ATM withdrawals, debit-card purchases or electronic payments. Term also known as, "bouncing."

** **Overdraft fee** – A fee charged for having a negative balance in a bank account.

Owe - be in debt; "She owes me $200"; "The thesis owes much to his adviser"; be obliged to pay or repay.

Own - have ownership or possession of; "He owns three houses in Florida"; "How many cars does she have?"

Parent - a father or mother; one who begets or one who gives birth to or nurtures and raises a child; a relative who plays the role of guardian; bring up; "raise a family"; "bring up children."

Payoff - the final payment of a debt. A recompense for worthy acts or retribution for wrongdoing; "the wages of sin is death"; "virtue is its own reward."

Planning - the act or process of drawing up plans or layouts for some project or enterprise; an act of formulating a program for a definite course of action; "the planning was more fun than the trip itself"; the cognitive process of thinking about what you will do in the event of something happening; "his planning for retirement was hindered by several uncertainties."

Play - engage in recreational activities rather than work; occupy oneself in a diversion.

* **Present Value** – sum of money payable at a future date. The current value of future cash payments when the payments are discounted by a rate that is a function of the interest rate. For example, the present value of $1,000 to be received in two years is $812 when the $1,000 is discounted at an annual rate of 11%. Conversely, $812 invested at an annual return of 11% would produce a sum of $1,000 in two years.

Property - something owned; any tangible possession that is owned by someone; "that hat is my property"; "he is a man of property."

Purchasing - the act of buying; "buying and selling fill their days"; "shrewd purchasing requires considerable knowledge."

* **Quick Ratio** - a relatively severe test of a family's liquidity and its ability to meet short-term obligations. The quick ratio is calculated by dividing all current assets with the exception of inventory by current liabilities. Inventory is excluded on the basis that it is the least liquid current asset. A relatively high quick ratio indicates conservative management and the ability to satisfy short-term obligations. This term is also known as acid-test ratio.

Record - anything (such as a document or a phonograph record or a photograph) providing permanent evidence of or information about past events; "the film provided a valuable record of stage techniques"; a document that can serve as legal evidence of a transaction; "they could find no record of the purchase"; make a record of; set down in permanent form.

Renting - the act of paying for the use of something (an apartment or house or car).

* **Retirement Plan** - in general, a pension is an arrangement to provide people with an income when they are no longer earning a regular income from employment. It is a tax deferred savings vehicle that allows for the tax-free accumulation of a fund for later use as a retirement income.

Rich – possessing material wealth.

Rule of 72 – a crafty calculation for figuring out the number of years it would take for your investment to double in value. The doubling of your money is based on the principle of compound interest. The computation is equal to the magic number 72 divided by the interest rate. For example, if the interest rate is 10%, then it will take 7.2 years for your monetary investment to double. This is assuming that you do not touch your funds in this case for 7.2 years.

Save - to keep up and reserve for personal or special use; spend less; buy at a reduced price; spend sparingly, avoid the waste of; "This move will save money"; "The less fortunate will have to economize now."

Savings - a fund of money put by as a reserve.

Savings Account - a bank account that accumulates interest.

Short-term - relating to or extending over a limited period; "short-run planning"; "a short-term lease"; "short-term credit."

Social Security - social welfare program in the U.S.; includes old-age and survivors insurance and some unemployment insurance and old-age assistance.

Spending - the act of disbursing money.

Starting a Business - the principal activity in your life that you do (want to do) to earn money; "he bought an industrial enterprise business"; "small mom-and-pop business."

Success – an event that accomplishes its intended purpose; a state of prosperity or fame; "he is enjoying great success."

Tangible Property - (of especially business assets) having physical substance and intrinsic monetary value; "tangible property like real estate"; "tangible assets such as machinery."

Tax – the charge against a citizen's person or property or activity for the support of government.

Variable (expenses) - something that is likely to vary; something that is subject to variation; "the utility bill is one variable to be considered."

Victory - a successful ending of a struggle or contest; "the general always gets credit for his army's victory"; "the agreement was a triumph for common sense."

Wealth - property that has economic utility: a monetary value or an exchange value; an abundance of material possessions and resources.

Win - a victory (as in a race or other competition); "he was happy to get the win"; win something through one's efforts; attain success or reach a goal; "The enterprise succeeded"; "We succeeded in getting tickets to the show"; "she struggled to overcome her handicap and won."

* **Working Capital** - the capital of a business that is used in its day-to-day trading operations, calculated as the current assets minus the current liabilities.

Zeal - excessive fervor to do something or accomplish some end; "he had an absolute zeal for financial liberty"; a feeling of strong eagerness (usually in favor of a person or cause); "they were imbued with a revolutionary ardor"; "he felt a kind of religious zeal."

Index

E

F

G

I

L

M

N

O

P

Table of Figures

Note-taking Sheet

Things to ponder in the near future

Record your comments here

Key Words, Tips or Phrases	Notes to process later	Page #
Things to Recall day(s) later		
Things to Recite later		
Things to Reflect on later		
Things to Review later		
Things to Recap much later		

Meet Cynthia Elliott, C.P.A.

Process 12: The ABCs in Cynthia's hand

Cynthia Elliott's life is centered on the constant need to obtain more knowledge in the field of personal financial management in order to pass the information on to others in dire financial need. As a Certified Public Accountant (CPA), she understands the pure essence of budgeting and saving as well as using the tools in one's life. Based on her education with a Masters of Business Administration in Finance, Ms. Elliott is quite capable of convincing individuals on how to implement the fun-filled techniques that she has personally established.

Her willingness to volunteer shows that she is able to produce age appropriate tools for all family members involved. With her personal experiences, she has empowered parents & their children to put into action what they have learned and to take charge of their finances. From her previous publications and course work, it is clear that she wants to improve the standards of individuals of which are necessary to climbing that financial ladder. The road map of *ABCs that make cent$* is to fine tune the families who want greatly to learn how to set up a well-defined plan that has been proven from past class participants. Ms. Elliott's background speaks volumes for herself; she is an expert in the field of finances. Her goal is to plant a seed and reward others.

Cynthia currently resides in Memphis, TN and has lived in New York, Florida, Texas and Georgia. Cynthia is an active member (> 15 years) of Cummings Street Baptist Church where she is dedicated to the Usher's and Children's Ministry. In addition to her commitment of assisting others in the community, her favorite pass time is playing the piano, bowling, skating and playing "Payday or Monopoly" board games with her daughter. Allow Cynthia's <u>hand</u> of expertise to provide the ***ABCs** that make cent$, a* foundation towards smart and purposeful spending.

CPSIA information can be obtained at www.ICGtesting.com
Printed in the USA
LVOW072108100212

268105LV00001BB/6/P